Marriage is a

Dedicated to making your marriage a life-long journey of joy and success.

Marriage is a Four-Letter Word

Copyright © 2015 Dr. Brian T. Hargis Th. D., D. Min., M. Div., B.A.

ISBN 978-0-9895513-2-8

Printed in the United States of America

Published by Blacksmith LLC
Fayetteville, NC
www.BlacksmithPublishing.com

Direct inquiries and/or orders to the above web address.

All rights reserved. Except for use in review, no portion of this book may be reproduced in any form without the express written permission from the publisher.

All Scripture quotations and references are from the text of the Authorized King James Version of the Bible. Any deviations therefrom were not intentional.

Professional photos by Melissa Esterline of Dayton, Ohio
www.melissaesterlinephotography.com (937) 266-4044

Contents

About the Author……………………………………...1

Chapter 1. Marriage is a Four-Letter Word …………………3

- Your Marital House
- Marital Leasing
- One Step at a Time
- Love Gives
- Drifting in Heart Before Drifting Apart

Chapter 2. Identifying Problems ……………………..19

- A Quick Fix?
- Get to the Root
- Major Issues

Chapter 3. Eliminating Problems ………………….. 33

- Make it Planned
- Make it Private
- Make it Positive
- Make it Productive
- Retaliator or Retreater
- Make it Prayerful

Chapter 4. Marriage Killers ……………………….49

- The D-Word
- Hate
- Name-Calling
- Put-Downs
- Profanity

Marriage is a Four-Letter Word

Chapter 5. Start Right, Stay Right, Finish Right ....…...67

- Law #1: You Reap What You Sow
- Law #2: You Reap Later Than You Sow
- Law #2: You Reap More Than You Sow
- Law #4: You Reap According to How You Sow
- We Didn't Start Right. Now What?

Chapter 6. Society's View of Marriage............................81

- What is Marriage?
- What Happened?
- The Seven-Year Itch
- Values

Chapter 7. The Missing Family Table…………………..93

- The Family Table
- Table Time
- Love & Lead
- Appreciate
- Sing
- Pray
- Communicate
- Rational
- Teamwork
- Manners
- Responsibilities
- Commit

Contents

Chapter 8. Improving the Marital Foxhole...................…...109

- Understanding Roles
- Providing Security
- Psychological Security
- Sexual Security
- Financial Security

Chapter 9. Reasonable Rules for Raising Rug Rats……..133

- Keeping Your Bed Private
- Keeping Your Bedroom Private
- Don't Argue in Front of Your Children
- Don't Argue with Your Children
- Ensure That Your No Means No
- Lights Out
- Affection
- Vicarious
- Forcing a Square Peg into a Round Hole
- Negative Influence
- Play Often
- Boys Need a Man
- Allow Children to Experience the Joy of the Ministry

Chapter 10. Forgive and Forget………………..………..165

- Forgiving
- Forgetting
- The Fault Box

Index…………………………………………………...…….179

Marriage is a Four-Letter Word

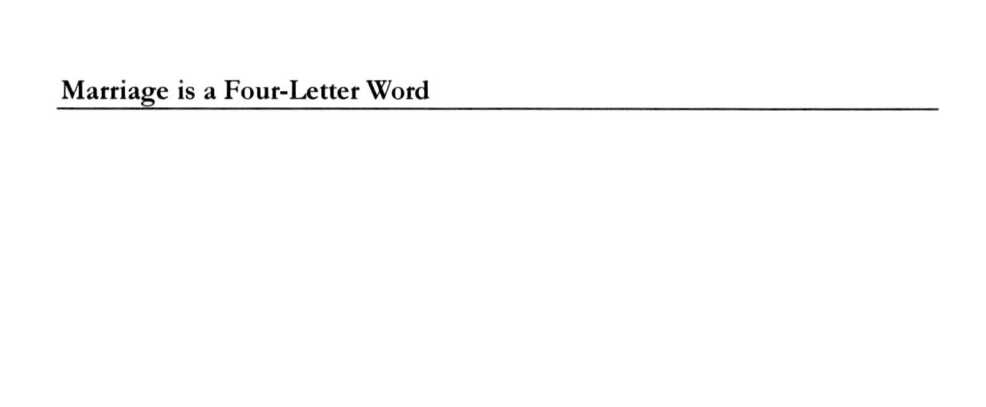

About the Author

Brian Hargis serves as a Chaplain to the U.S. Army but his journey began in 1991 when he enlisted in the Army to jump from airplanes. After fulfilling his active-duty obligation, Brian transitioned to the Ohio Army National Guard and was assessed to become a Green Beret with 2nd Battalion, 19th Special Forces Group (Airborne).

Brian was selected for U.S. Army Special Forces training from 1995-1996, and upon completion of language school and graduation he served as a Special Forces Engineer on ODA 955. By 2003 he had deployed numerous times to several different countries on peacekeeping and foreign internal defense missions. After back-to-back missions in Hungary, Kuwait and Kosovo, Brian switched fields and became a Senior Drill Sergeant in the Army Reserves, graduating with honors.

After two successful years training Soldiers, Brian returned to Special Forces and was promoted to Master Sergeant (E-8). For the next two years he evaluated, trained, supervised and mentored several hundred Soldiers to become qualified SF *Green Berets,* many of whom are serving in the U.S. Army today.

Serving in the U.S. Army National Guard and the Army Reserves afforded Brian the opportunity to have a civilian career. Beginning in 1999 until 2003, he served his community as a police officer for the City of Dayton, Ohio while attending seminary and teaching in local church ministries. In August of 2003, Brian resigned from the Police Department and entered full-time Christian service where he was ordained and ministered as an Assistant Pastor, Youth Minister, hospital and jail Chaplain for the following six years.

Completing his Master of Divinity in 2007, he recognized God's direction to become an Army Chaplain to bring military members and their families the message of hope. Brian surrendered to the call and has served with numerous military units, which included deployments for Operation Enduring Freedom and Operation Resolute Support. Additionally he has served as senior pastor to military congregations at Fort Drum, NY, Fort Polk, LA and Fort Bragg, NC.

Brian still jumps from airplanes in the U.S. Army, but his real passions are preaching, teaching, counseling, developing leaders and building ministries. Brian is married to Tracy of Dayton, Ohio, since 1992. They have three sons, Jordan, Izak and Levi. Free moments are spent enjoying each other and living life to the fullest with the Lord as the center.

For additional information, you may contact the author by e-mail: brianhargis1@gmail.com.

Chapter 1

Marriage is a Four-Letter Word

It's no hidden secret. It's no mystery. It's no deep revelation or epiphany. Marriage is a four-letter word: it's W-O-R-K.

Say *WORK*.

Say it again.

Say it enough times to get used to it.

If you want a healthy, happy, life-lasting marriage, it will take some work. Working to communicate effectively and keep the marriage healthy is not always glamorous but it has to be done. As an example, many people love what they do for a career, and to these people the work involved is second nature.[1] On the other hand, some people hate their job and dread getting up every Monday morning to go to it. In the same sense, the perception of work within a marriage is dependent upon the love between the spouses. When you love, more importantly when you are *in* love, the work involved in the marriage becomes part of life. It's a term that I call **"keeping the love alive."**

"*Work*" is found 420 times in the Scriptures making it a significant topic. It first appears in Scripture three times referring to the work of the triune Creator:

> "And on the seventh day God ended His **work** which He had made; and He rested on the seventh day from all His **work** which He had made. And God blessed the seventh day, and sanctified it: because that in it He had rested from all His **work** which God created and made." Genesis 2:2-3

Such complex, inconceivable beauty that we enjoy every day didn't evolve by itself over the course of billions of years. It was brought about by the careful *work* of an intelligent designer—the Creator, God Almighty.

In the same sense, marriage will not magically evolve into something beautiful and permanent with time. It must be deliberately and carefully built with each block that is laid in its foundation. There must be some labor involved to maintain it. If your marriage is not structurally strong, if the foundation is weak, or if you cease in the upkeep, then your marriage will decay, collapse and fade away.

Your Marital House

Compare your marriage to purchasing a new house. Without consistent care and yearly maintenance, your house will eventually fall apart! You need to apply paint every so often, repair the toilet, stain the deck and seal the driveway. You have to replace filters, fixtures, faucets and fans. If you fail to maintain your house, you'll have nothing but problem after problem in the years ahead.

Go ahead and avoid the upkeep. Cut corners on repairs and see what happens. Stop mowing the grass and flushing the toilet. Ignore that leaky faucet, the squeaky garage door, the crack in the ceiling and the loose handrail to the basement. Never mind with the air filters and the salt for your water softener. Oh, and the roof that needs new shingles, let that one slide too. Let it all go and just wait a few months.

It won't be long before you realize that the damage done and the subsequent price of repairs will cost you far more down the road than you could ever have imagined. In the space of just a few short years, the value of your once-beautiful home will be drastically reduced by thousands of dollars.

Silly isn't it? I mean, who in their right mind would purchase a home but not put work and effort into maintaining it, right? Wrong! Many homeowners

Chapter 1. Marriage is a Four-Letter Word

set out with great intentions and high expectations for their home but life happens and care slips through the cracks with each passing year.

Take a walk around your neighborhood and you'll find that one dilapidated home with the gutter falling off and the grass knee-high. Even wealthier communities that have a list of neighborhood violations (for 'offenses' such as untrimmed hedges or a displaying a sign in the front lawn) will most likely have that one house in violation of a city ordinance.[2]

What happened to the home over the years? Where did it go wrong? For starters, someone stopped pouring care into it. Somebody stopped putting time and effort into it. Something changed in this area, and that *something* is called *work*.

Maintaining your own home is not always glamorous or exciting…but it is always necessary. I don't mind making repairs and upgrading my home. I'm not the type to pour hundreds of hours into landscaping and gardening like many neighbors, but I'm satisfied with the time and effort we dedicate to making our little home our castle, a place of refuge for our family. I've realized over time that it's far better to maintain it then to play catch-up in repairs.

Your marital house is a long-term investment that pays off in accordance with how much you put into it: The more you put into it, the more you'll get out.

Marital Leasing

A problem that many couples face is that they value their marriage about as much as they value rental property. There's no long-term investment in rental property because there's no long-term ownership – no commitment.

Their marriage is like a one-year lease agreement that has to be reconsidered every twelve months. If the location is wrong, if the cost is too high, if the size is too big or small, if their career takes them away, or if they just don't like what they've gotten themselves into… they'll simply walk away and look for another place to take up residency. Some call it separation or an annulment. Others call it divorce.

Marriage is a Four-Letter Word

The reason why many couples walk away from an otherwise workable and salvageable marriage is that their internal lease has expired. The lifetime commitment they promised at the altar of marriage was to them (in their minds) negotiable. It wasn't permanent. It wasn't life lasting. It was a thought with no lifetime commitment. Their promise of "*for better or for worse until death us do part*" had limitations.[3] So, for many spouses, getting out of their marital commitment, which took place in the presence of witnesses, is as simple as walking away from a rental lease.[4]

Then there's the care and maintenance of the rental property. When the main sewage line clogs, who comes to unclog it? When the garage door needs replaced, who replaces it? When the front door falls off the hinges, who repairs it? When the walls need paint, who paints them? It's typically not the renter who is responsible – it's the property owner. I mean, why fix it if it's not yours?

The renters have no long-term investment because there's no lifetime commitment. They have no intention of living in the residence forever. They rent for the sake of convenience and flexibility.

For the first seven years of our marriage, my wife and I rented four apartments. I was a young enlisted man in the U.S. Army, so renting was our obvious choice. We enjoyed our flexibility. It was easy to come and go as we pleased. We did not intend to rent for that long, but we weren't established enough financially to purchase a home. Although we signed lease after lease, we could've walked away at any time and the only loss incurred would've been our deposit.

In 1999 we purchased our first home in Dayton, Ohio. Eight years later, we sold and moved into a larger home in the neighboring community of Beavercreek. In 2009 we moved to Watertown, New York and purchased a more spacious home. In 2012 we moved to Leesville, LA and in 2013 we moved to Raeford, NC. Soon we will pack up and move again....and continue this trend every two to three years. Each move has required a larger truck. Each move required more cardboard boxes and packing tape! Each move required more movers.

What I realized was that in over 20 years of marriage we acquired a lot of stuff along the way! To pick up and move now is painful… but we did it and we'll do it again in the future. It takes work.

You see, it's more difficult to move around when you have more invested. It's more complicated. There's more risk involved because there's more to damage and lose.

Think about your marriage and ask yourself these questions:

- Am I a renter or an owner?
- Do I have a renter's attitude about my marriage, or an owner's attitude?
- Do I take ownership and responsibility for my marriage?
- Am I committed to marriage temporarily or for life?
- How much work am I investing in my marriage?
- What have I invested in my marriage today?

When you approach your marriage with the attitude of lifetime ownership, and not that of a monthly renter, you will have an investor's mindset that says, "I'm in it to win it and I will finish this marriage marathon!"

Pour some care and attention into it today by identifying and making repairs as needed….then work at maintaining it.

One Step at a Time

My favorite place to climb is in the middle of nowhere, tucked away in the backwoods of the West Virginia Appalachians.[5] It's found at the heart of a one stop sign country town called Seneca Rocks. In the last two decades, I've had the privilege to coach at least 25 new climbers to the 250' vertical summit of this pristine granite playground.

From the parking lot at the base of Seneca Rocks, one stands in awe at the jetting plates of rock that have pushed through the earth's crust and into the

Marriage is a Four-Letter Word

blue sky, much like the Flat Irons of Boulder, Colorado. Nearly all of my first-time climbers take one look at the breathtaking summit and remark with astonishment, *"Wow!"* followed by a matter-of-fact, *"There's no way that I can climb that!"*

After hiking the one-mile trail and scampering the ledges to where we begin our training, reality reinforces their fears. I've heard it all…

"I've never climbed before."

"I can't climb to the top of this."

"It ain't gonna' happen!"

"You've got to be kidding me!"

What they fail to see are all the numerous hand and footholds in the rock that are right in front of their face. To seasoned climbers, they're known as *bomber holds* – hand holds big enough to hang on all day long! So, to help eliminate their fear and enable the newbies to focus on the task at hand, I direct their attention to the short climb directly in front of them, not to the continuous vertical wall that's hovering 200' above them.

> **Climber**: "Brian, you're crazy to bring me here! I can't climb to the top of this."
>
> **Me**: "Quit being so negative! This is an easy 5.4 route.[6] Don't look at it as an obstacle – look at it as an opportunity! It will be fun. Do you see that ledge 10' above our heads? Can you climb to that?"
>
> **Climber**: "Maybe. I don't know, but I definitely can't climb to the top!"
>
> **Me:** "Forget about the top! Just focus on the ledge above your head and climb to it, okay? I've got you on belay and you're not going anywhere even if you slip. Trust me and trust your equipment."
>
> **Climber**: "Alright, I'll give it a shot."
>
> **Me**: "Climb on, climber!"

We begin to climb. A few moments later, the ledge is reached and it wasn't

Chapter 1. Marriage is a Four-Letter Word

the impossible mission that they envisioned after all. With their confidence building along the granite route, the same process is repeated until, before you know it, we are delivering high-fives and yodeling jubilant exclamations while standing on the summit some 250' above where we started.

How did they get there? Was it all at once? Was it one giant leap? Of course not. They got there by focusing on the immediate and taking one small step at a time.

> "The journey of a thousand miles begins with a single step."
> ~ Lao-Tzu [7]

In the classic movie *What About Bob?* Dr. Leo Marvin delivered his solution for overcoming obstacles to his patient, Bob Wiley (played by actor Bill Murray) using a counseling method that he called ***baby steps*** – small steps taken to achieve success. A very comical production indeed, yet the *baby steps* method rings true for achieving most anything in life – including your marriage.

When you see a strong, healthy marriage, please don't assume that it magically developed the moment they said their wedding vows to each other. Strong marriages take years of work and are forged through adversity that requires consistent, calculated, planned and deliberate *baby steps.* That's what enables them to go the distance.

For those of you that have experienced or are experiencing hardships and problems in your marriage, stop looking at your mountain of circumstances and allowing your mind to think that it's impossible to go forward. Stop looking at the vertical walls of setback. Stop looking at the top of the mountain and developing reasons why you can't make it. Instead, focus on what's directly in front of you – the things you can control and affect right now, on a daily basis. Put some work to your words and take small *baby steps* of progress.

GOD CAN TURN OBSTACLES INTO OPPORTUNITIES

Allow God to be in between you and your marital circumstances, instead of your circumstances between you and God. Those obstacles are Gods opportunities for miracles.

Love Gives

A marriage that has commitment takes work. I challenge you to not look at the word *"work"* negatively but rather to view it as a positive word that produces positive results.

The saying, *"You bring about what you think about"* can work both negatively and positively. When you think about the work invested in your marriage in a positive manner, it will positively produce positive results! When you're in love you won't mind the work that you invest in the relationship nor will you realize how much work you are investing. It's not as if you whip out a notebook and keep track of it as if you're counting calories for a diet! That's not what it's about.

As a spiritual analogy, consider the Biblical perspective of eternal redemption. The Word of God clearly states that you are saved through faith and not by works.

> *"For by grace are ye saved through faith; and that not of yourselves: it is the* gift *of God: **Not of works**, lest any man should boast."* Ephesians 2:8-9

> **Actions speak louder than words**

God's salvation of my soul and forgiveness of my sins put a love in my heart that propels me to live for Him. I'm not attempting to perform good works so that I can be forgiven and, hopefully, *make it* into Heaven. My daily displays of good works are an outward product of an inward faith. I live my life for God because I want to, not because I have to!

> *"… shew me thy faith without thy works, and I will shew thee my faith by my works."* James 2:18

If your life has been changed by the Lord Jesus Christ then you should have an internal desire to produce good works in your marriage.

Chapter 1. Marriage is a Four-Letter Word

Why?

1. Because it pleases Jesus Christ who shed His blood to redeem your soul.[8]

2. Because you are a recipient of nine fruits of the Spirit, therefore your love is demonstrated by your works.[9]

The term, "*actions speak louder than words*" describes the steps necessary to be confident that your spouse loves you. They demonstrate it in their actions. True love causes you to give. You'll give of your time, talent and treasure. All the "work" involved will be a byproduct of your love and you won't think twice about it. It comes naturally with love and you can't help it. In contrast, love that is dying or dead has lost its enthusiasm in the relationship, thus losing its desire to give.

> **You can say the words and talk the talk, but real love is demonstrated when it walks the walk.**

Indicators that your marital love is dying is when:

- Birthdays no longer mean that much and you don't put forth good effort to make them special.
- Anniversaries are just another year gone by. The romantic getaway is outdated.
- Dates to dinner and a movie are rare.
- Baseball is more important than back massages.
- Computers are more important than cuddling.
- Facebook is more important than face time.
- Shopping is more exciting than sex.
- Hunting is more important than hugs.
- Special events are no longer special.

What kind of life is that? Sounds miserable! When the love is alive, you'll want to make your spouse's birthday special. You'll want to celebrate your anniversary. You'll want to spend quality time together. You'll plan and look forward to intimacy.

Marriage is a Four-Letter Word

Perhaps you have watched a sports game when someone from the audience hung a sheet from the stands or held a sign in front of the camera with the well-known verse written in bold letters: JOHN 3:16.[10] It's the most famous verse in the Bible and it's the epitome of God's love. The first nine words of the verse show us that God's unending love propelled Him to give something extremely special:

> *"For God so **loved** the world that He **gave** his only begotten Son, that whosoever believeth in him should not perish, but have everlasting life."* John 3:16

Love caused God to give. His own example is proof positive that love gives! Any work associated with the upkeep of a marriage doesn't matter because love gives, love forgives, love lives, it thrives and survives the test of time. Love is greater than faith and hope combined![11]

Look at a few additional supporting Scripture to show that God loves us, and His love compelled Him to give...

> *"And this is the record, that God hath **given** to us eternal life, and this life is in his Son."* 1 John 5:11

> *"Grace be to you and peace from God the Father, and from our Lord Jesus Christ, Who **gave** himself for our sins, that he might deliver us from this present evil world, according to the will of God and our Father:"* Galatians 1:3-4

> *"Who **gave** himself for us, that he might redeem us from all iniquity, and purify unto himself a peculiar people, zealous of good works."* Titus 2:14

> *"And walk in love, as Christ also hath loved us, and hath **given** himself for us an offering and a sacrifice to God for a sweetsmelling savour."* Ephesians 5:2

One of the problems we have with marriage today is that society's definition and ideas of what love is have been blurred.[12] You won't find real love by reading romance novels, watching CNN, *Oprah, Dr. Phil, Jerry Springer*, or

Desperate Housewives. Real love is of God, because God is love.

> *"Beloved, let us love one another: for **love is of God**; and every one that loveth is born of God, and knoweth God. He that loveth not knoweth not God; for **God is love**."* 1 John 4:7-8

So if you are searching for a deeper understanding of what the essence of true love in marriage is all about, then here's my advice: develop a strong relationship with love itself – God.

- The more communication you'll have instead of conflict.
- The more intimacy you'll have instead of disinterest.
- The more you'll understand about a love that compels you to give.
- The more of God that you have inside, the more up days you'll have instead of down days.

One thing is for sure…you can't be *up* on God and be *down* on your spouse. It just doesn't work that way. You can't be walking with the Lord and *hating* on your spouse. Remember, God is ultimate love, so you can't be in love with the Lord – in harmonious fellowship with Him – while harboring resentment or anger for another person. You can, however, be a hypocrite. You can fuss with your family on the way to church, and praise Jesus when you get there. That type of behavior may fool others, but it doesn't fool the family.

In essence, if your relationship with God is close, so, too, will *your part* of your relationship with your spouse be. Notice I said *your part* because that doesn't mean that your spouse will automatically fall into the same groove. It simply means that *your part* will be in check regardless of how they respond.

Drifting in Heart before Drifting Apart

Just for a moment, I want you to concentrate on the time when you were first dating, courting and falling in love with your spouse. Remember those affectionate acts of appreciation that were shown to you? Remember the small tokens of gratitude that were given to you? Remember the things that you gave up, gave in, or gave over because of your love?

Marriage is a Four-Letter Word

Would you admit that you were much more giving during that courting phase? In general terms, wherever she wanted to eat, that's where you went. Whatever she wanted to watch, that's what you watched. You embraced servanthood, one towards another. You both shared. You both gave.

> *"Submitting yourselves one to another in the fear of God."*
> Ephesians 5:21

Are you still looking out for each other? What changed over time? What happened to the love?

An elderly couple was driving down an old country road to their farmhouse, the same country road that they've driven down throughout their 50 years of their marriage.

The woman looked over at her husband and said, "Honey, remember way back in the earlier years of our marriage, we used to travel up and down this old country road in our pickup truck and I used to snuggle up beside you and you'd put your arm around me? The wind would blow through the windows and we'd enjoy the scenery together. Ah, we were so in love. Now the years have gone by and you're way over there and I'm way over here... what happened?"

The husband, with his eyes fastened on that old country road and his left hand on the steering wheel, replied, "I never moved."

In a marriage that drifts apart, someone first begins drifting away at heart before it's ever demonstrated in an action. It may have happened like this...
Husband: "Hey babe, where would you like to eat tonight?"
   Wife: "Wherever you want dear."
   Husband: "It really doesn't matter to me. Why don't you choose?"
   Wife: "I don't really care. Anywhere is fine."
   Husband: "Anywhere? I'm not really sure what I'm hungry for."
   Wife: "Well, I chose last time. Why don't you just pick somewhere?"
   Husband: "Alright. How about Outback Steakhouse?"
   Wife: "Hmm. I'm not really in the mood for steak, but that's fine."
   Husband: "Okay. How about Bob Evans?"

Chapter 1. Marriage is a Four-Letter Word

Wife: "Didn't we just go there last week?"

Husband: "Sheeesh. You pick a place."

Wife: "Why am I the one that has to always make the decision? Let's just go to Bob Evans then."

Husband: "You don't sound too enthused about it. Seriously, I don't really care where we go."

Wife: "Why don't you care? Aren't I important to you?"

Husband: "Of course you're important to me, but every time I choose a place, you don't want to go there."

Wife: "I never said I didn't want to go there."

Husband: "Yes you did."

Wife: "No I didn't."

Husband: "Yes you did."

Wife: "No I didn't."

Husband: "What did you say then?"

Wife: "What I said was that I didn't care where we went. I'm just not in the mood for steak, but it's okay."

Husband: "Fine. Forget it then."

Wife: "Fine. I will forget it."

Husband: "Fine then."

Wife: "Yeah, fine."

Wife: "You know what? I don't want to go now anyways!"

Husband: "Well, you started it."

Wife: "Started what? I didn't start anything. You did!" Husband: "You're the one that can't make up your mind. It would've been better if we wouldn't have even gone out."

Wife: "Well, next time you can go by yourself then."

Husband: "That'd be great. At least I'd know where to go."

Wife: "I'll tell you where you can go. You can go to #@*%!"

If you know this to be true then I'm sure you are smiling right now. Perhaps you have been there once or twice.

This type of communication is not uncommon among married couples and it happens more frequently than you might imagine. One thing is for sure about the couple illustrated here: their relationship didn't start off like that years ago. Somewhere along the line of time, there was a drifting away in heart before it ever came out in the words. They stopped identifying issues that caused arguments, and began replacing effective communication by the ineffective.

> **Communication breakdowns are a leak in the marital roof.**

Communication breakdowns like this are the leak in the marital roof. A little repair now will prevent it from growing into a water-damaged labyrinth of mold and decay. Will the marital roof cave in today? No. Not likely. It will take a while, drip by drip.

The drips will become a slow but steady stream as the hole enlarges itself. Eventually there will be a collapse. This couple's leak can be repaired before it's too late, but it will take some – what? That's right: Work.

WORK – The four-letter word of marriage:

- Work to eliminate the identified problems.
- Work to avoid arguments with your spouse.
- Work to listen twice as much as you talk.
- Work to avoid trigger words and phrases.
- Work to maintain your cool and composure.
- Work to find happy mediums among the differences.
- Work to please your spouse more than yourself.
- Work to keep your eyes only on your spouse.
- Work to spend time doing what they want to do.
- Work to incorporate some of your spouse's convictions.
- Work to give up some of your own convictions.
- Work to be an investor in your marriage.
- Work to keep from drifting in heart.
- Work to keep the love alive.
- Work to recognize the issues before they become problems.

How to do it? Through:

- Self-EVALUATION
- Daily DEDICATION
- Personal MOTIVATION
- Biblical SATURATION
- Radical TRANSFORMATION
- Effective COMMUNICATION

Marriage is a Four-Letter Word

Chapter 2

Identifying Problems

You can't fix a problem until you identify what's causing it. Marital issues cannot be fixed until you first identify and understand what the problems are.

While on one of the deployments to Afghanistan, I called home and my wife told me that the SUV wouldn't start. The conversation went like this:

Tracy: "Yeah, I don't know what's wrong. I tried to start it but it just won't start."

Me: "What happened when you turned the key?"

Tracy: "Nothing."

Me: "Did it make any sound like it was trying to start? Like Rrrrr-rrrrr-rrrrr?"

Tracy: "Nope."

Me: "Did it make a clicking noise when you turned the key?"

Tracy: "No. None of that. It's completely dead."

Me: "Hmm. It sounds like the battery is dead, but it can't be the battery because I just bought it six months ago! Maybe it's the alternator. Maybe you have a loose battery connection."

Tracy: "I checked the cables and they seemed tight."

Me: "Sorry babe but you'll have to take the battery out and have it tested at AutoZone. Fortunately, it's still under warranty. If it's not the battery, then it's probably the alternator."

Marriage is a Four-Letter Word

The next day...

>Tracy: "Hey *hon*, I took the battery to AutoZone and it was completely dead. They recharged it and I put it in the SUV. It started right up."
>
>Me: "Great! Glad it wasn't the alternator."
>
>Tracy: "I found out what the problem was though."
>
>Me: "You did? What was it?"
>
>Tracy: "Izak left the interior light on. It must've been on for a couple of days because we haven't driven it in a while."
>
>Me: "Aha! So that was the problem."

You see, the real problem was not that the SUV didn't start. That's a symptom of the problem; a byproduct of the real issue. The *real problem* was that the battery was dead – which prevented the vehicle from starting. And the *real reason* was because the dome light was left on and it drained the battery. On the surface, the car was disabled, but under the hood was actually where the real issue was.

If your marriage is dead or dying, that's a symptom of the real problem. Dig deeper and you'll find that your marital "battery" is dead. Dig a little deeper still and you'll discover other reasons for a dead "battery." You'll need a marital jumpstart, a charge or possibly a new battery.

You don't just call the scrap yard and ask them to come tow it away. That's what you do for an old clunker that has been rusting away in the barn for 30 years. You identify the problem to fix it.

A Quick Fix

When you get a headache, do you seek to identify the problem or just take Tylenol to make your headache go away? Your headache is your body's response to an issue that has triggered your brain that you have a problem requiring attention. Your brain develops an ache in your head to inform you. Hence, the word *headache*....but the headache is not the problem; it's a symptom.

Chapter 2. Identifying Problems

The problem may be that you're dehydrated. You may need to eat something. You may need to go outside and get some fresh air. You may need to lay down for a few minutes. You may be under stress that requires you to temporarily walk away and relax. You may just need a few more hours of sleep at night.

When the brain sends signals in the form of a headache, the average person doesn't identify and treat the problem.

Instead of figuring out why we have a headache, we treat the symptom by popping a *Motrin, Tylenol* or *Aleve* to make the headache go away. It's a quick fix. It's easier than trying to figure out what is wrong. We've been programmed to pop a pill and forget it.

It's like buying the next waist size on a pair of pants. We will blame our waistline on many things but the increase in our waist size is not the real problem – it is a byproduct of the problem. The real problem is not the increase in size but the need to push away from the table.

You can't treat internal issues with external methods

We all know of someone who had weight loss surgery and lost a considerable amount of weight, only to gain it all back again within a year or two. What went wrong? What happened? What happened was that the *real* problem was never changed. The symptom of the problem was treated, but the real issue was not resolved. The outside may have been altered, but the inside never changed.

This type of thinking that I'm introducing to you is common sense that goes unrecognized in everyday life – and especially in marriages. Couples try to change the external all the time without ever changing the internal. So many hurting spouses have issues that they attempt to hide behind a smile and a masquerade – but you can't treat internal marital issues with external methods![1]

As a pastor and counselor, let me just say that the only long-lasting, life-lasting internal and external victory you will ever achieve does not come through plastic surgery, a gym membership, a dream home, money in your savings account or a cruise vacation to the Bahamas.[2] It comes through a daily

Marriage is a Four-Letter Word

relationship with Christ Jesus. It is internal satisfaction that is manifested outwardly by love and appreciation for your spouse, thus keeping the love alive.

If you argue all the time, the problem is not that you argue – that's a symptom. There's an underlying reason why you argue.

If you say, *"He doesn't listen to me,"* or *"She always talks down to me,"* or *"I can't trust her with*_____*(money, men, the Mall, etc.),"* then you are stating symptoms of the problem, but you're not truly identifying anything other than the fact that you both can't effectively communicate.

In your marriage, decide not to dwell on the symptoms of problems, but rather to identify what the real problems are so that you can eliminate them. As Arnold Schwarzenegger would say, "terminate" them.

Get to the Root

Have you ever tried to eliminate weeds in your yard but were unsuccessful? I've battled many a lawn with every type of weed killer and pesticide on the market, only to have them grow back. The very best method that I've found to successfully eliminate the annoying weeds is to do it the hard way – on hand and knees with a weed plucker.

If you don't get underground and pull the root out, the weed will grow back.

A real counseling session…

> **Counselor:**[3] "So you say your husband doesn't listen to you. Why do you feel that he doesn't listen to you?"
>
> Wife: "Because he walks away every time I try to discuss something important. It gets irritating that he doesn't listen to me."
>
> **Counselor: "Why do you believe that he walks away?"**
>
> Wife: "I don't know. He just says that he doesn't want to deal with it."
>
> **Counselor: "Deal with what?"**
>
> Wife: "Things that he doesn't think are important to him. Nothing seem to be

Chapter 2. Identifying Problems

important to him! He doesn't care anymore."

Counselor: "Why do you think that he doesn't care?"

Wife: "He doesn't do anything. All he cares about is himself."

Counselor: "Why is that?"

Wife: "He's very independent. I don't think he really needs me or wants me."

Counselor: "Is there a reason why you believe that he is so independent?

Wife: "Well, he has been gone a lot for the military. When he's back it just seems like all we do is fight."

Now we've gotten somewhere as we peel back the layers. We've identified the heart of the issue and can identify that the husband has some hurdles to overcome so that he can effectively communicate with his wife. Realize, though, that there are *ALWAYS* two sides to the story. Both of them need to work at communicating effectively.

To the husband;

Counselor: "Your wife says that you don't listen to her. What's your take on that?"

Husband: "I listen to her, but I'm not going to tolerate her talking down to me. It's annoying."

Counselor: "How does she talk down to you?'

Husband: "She makes derogatory remarks and it seems as if I can do nothing right. I'm not going to let her talk to me that way."

Counselor: "What remarks does she make?"

Husband: "She calls me names and it irritates me. She says that I'm a sorry, inconsiderate father to the kids. Stuff like that."

Counselor: "Why do you think that she call you names?"

Husband: "I don't know. Maybe because her family fights like that all

Marriage is a Four-Letter Word

the time – yelling and getting on each other's nerves. Why are you asking me all these questions?"

Counselor: "I'm trying to get to the root of the issues. You're helping me understand by painting the big picture. So what do you do when she calls you names? Fight back, walk away, and clam up?"

Husband: "I just walk away and try to ignore her. It's either that or do something I'll regret."

Counselor: "Walking away is one method of dealing with her. It's an acceptable when done correctly, but why not just calmly talk to her about the problems? Have you expressed your feelings to her – the things you just told me?

Husband: "Heck no. She doesn't listen. It's just too much work."

Counselor: "What is 'too much work?"

Husband: "Talking to her. Communicating. My life was much simpler while I was gone on deployment or when I'm at work. When I tell soldiers to do something, they do it. There's no whining about it. I don't get their attitudes. No feedback. No backtalk. No criticism. I can't even ask what she bought at Walmart yesterday without getting in an argument about money."

Counselor: "I sense that you feel less of a leader at home than at work."

Husband: "True. It's much more difficult now than ever before. There's no respect."

Counselor: "Do you realize that walking away and ignoring your wife won't solve your problems?"

Husband: "Sure but it's better than doing something stupid and her calling the cops on me."

Finally, we are at the root of the issue. Everything up to this point was just a symptom of the problem. Both the husband and wife are running away from issues instead of dealing with them directly. The husband doesn't know of any stress-coping mechanism of which to use in communicating with his wife. He feels like he's not in control at home, and work makes

Chapter 2. Identifying Problems

him more comfortable. This is common among military members with multiple deployments.

In this situation, perhaps he would face the issues if he felt like he was more in control of the conversations. The wife tends to allow her anger to surface and it's manifested in verbal killers of the marriage, which encourages his desire to walk away. He cannot be the loving leader if he has no one to lead, and without tools to communicate, it will be extremely challenging.

Counselor: "Marriage is a four-letter word. Do you know what that is?"

Husband: "Hell?"

Counselor: (chuckle) "I've heard that a time or two."

Husband: "Is it love?"

Counselor: "Well, it sure requires love to survive the test of time. Love causes you to give and appreciate. However, the correct answer is work. W-o-r-k. You have to work at it. What's the best characteristic that you can work on when your wife begins to discuss something with you?"

Husband: "My anger?"

Counselor: "Yes, but anger is a byproduct, a reaction, rather a symptom of and an emotion evoked by what the real issue is. How about start by listening? Not saying a word but just hearing her out. Let her vent. Think about this….God gave you two ears and one mouth so that you can listen twice as much as you speak. So don't just *hear* what she says, but listen to *how* she says it and watch her body language that goes along with it. Can you try that?"

Husband: "I guess. She may not think that I'm listening. She may get mad or something."

Marriage is a Four-Letter Word

>**Counselor: "How could you show your wife that you are listening?"**

>Husband: "I don't know."

>**Counselor: "You can stop anything that you are doing, turn and direct your attention to her. You show appreciation and good communication when you turn and listen, and she may be surprised! The bottom line is…she wants your attention. What else could you do?"**

>Husband: "Stop walking away from her. She hates that."

>**Counselor: "Yep. Those are two great keys to get you started: listen without walking away."**

>Husband: "But she just goes on and on and on like a broken record."

>**Counselor: "Okay. We can deal with that. It's called passing the ball of communication. She'll need to learn it as well, but let me work with her a little more as I'm working with you. In the meantime, you work on you."**

Up to this point, the wife's perception was that her husband never listens to her. The husband perceived his wife as always talking down to him. We've broken some ground with the husband and, with consistent patience in counseling; it will begin to show in their relationship.

Your body language (facial expressions; nervous leg movement; nose-scratching, etc.) say more than your words. That's why you can hear the words, "I love you" or "I'm sorry," and feel like you are being lied to. What you actually say (context) is only 7% *of the message,* **but how you say it is 93%!**

Back to the wife…

>**Counselor: "Your husband said that one of the reasons he walks away is because you talk down to him. Could you explain what you think he means?"**

>Wife: "I don't talk down to him! You should see the way he treats me! If you only knew…"

>**Counselor: "Okay, okay, let's call a time out for a moment. I'm**

Chapter 2. Identifying Problems

simply relaying how your husband feels, so please realize that this is his perception, which may not be the reality. There are always two sides to every story. Do you call him names when you get upset?"

Wife: "Well... sometimes he makes me so angry that I do."

Counselor: "Why do you call him names?"

Wife: "Because he's inconsiderate and all he thinks about is himself."

Counselor: "If your husband considers you calling him names a form of talking down to him, what could you do to make him feel differently?"

Wife: "I could try to stop calling him names and yelling at him, but I just get so angry."

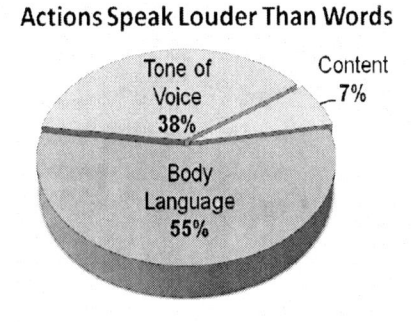

Actions Speak Louder Than Words

- Tone of Voice 38%
- Content 7%
- Body Language 55%

Counselor: "When you feel yourself getting angry, what should you do?"

Wife: "I don't know what to do. Walk away?"

Counselor: "Perhaps, temporarily, if it will keep you from saying something you shouldn't say. When your husband gets frustrated, he walks away... so if both of you walked away, it wouldn't solve the problems. That's what happens when two "retreaters" react. It would only create temporary peace, but frustration turned inside fosters bitterness, and bitterness becomes resentment. Besides the context of what you say, how might your form of communication make him want to walk away?"

Wife: "He says I don't ever shut-up... and I know I have a problem with it, but I like to talk"

Counselor: "Good. If you pass the ball of communication, and he works at opening up to you, you'll have effective communication. Let me say that you both have issues. You

Marriage is a Four-Letter Word

have issues and your husband has issues. Say this: "I have issues."

Wife: "I have issues."

Counselor: "Do you believe that you have issues?"

Wife: "Yes, I know I have to work on some things but he also has a lot of things that he needs to..."

Counselor: "Yes he certainly does, but I need you to focus on just you for the moment. Do you have issues to work on?"

Wife: "Yes, I do."

Counselor: "So you both have issues, but in order to resolve those issues, you both need to communicate effectively. Now what would you like your husband to do to better communicate with you?"

Wife: "He could stop and just listen to me when I have something to discuss."

Counselor: "Right. He needs to take time to do exactly that and I'll work with him on it. In the meanwhile, sum up everything we talked about so that you can communicate better."

Wife: "I can try not to get so upset and stop following him around the house, calling him names. I can also find a better time to talk about important issues."

Counselor: "Yes, that's a great start. Coordinate a convenient time for both of you to talk. Lastly, if you work on you, while your husband works on himself... it will work out, especially if you have a daily and personal relationship with God."

I once counseled a couple that argued so much during a premarital counseling session that I left them in the middle of an argument, went outside and selected a large rock. I took it inside and wrote **"Rock of Communication"** with a black Sharpie. On the other side, I wrote the rules:

1. You can only talk when you have the rock.
2. You can only listen when you don't have the rock.
3. Keep the message clear, concise and complete.

Chapter 2. Identifying Problems

I gave the rock to the couple, explained the rules and they used it for the rest of the session. Not only did it keep them from arguing, it facilitated listening and enhanced proper communication.

The couple kept the rock and continued to use it in private discussions. Today they are happily married and keep the rock – just in case!

Major Issues

It's without a doubt that poor communication is the largest threat to a marriage, yet ineffective communication is not the problem in itself – it's a symptom of the problem. Typically, the major issues that threaten a marriage are:

1. Current stressors (birth of a child, career change, new house, new automobile, deployment, relocation, death, health issues, professional discipline, legal issues, etc.).

2. Financial issues (debt, lack of money, re-financing, etc.).

3. Destructive behaviors (drug, alcohol, abuse of prescription medication, pornography, gambling and spending addictions, and other compulsive behaviors).

4. Sexual issues (infidelity, an STD, sexual frustration/ tension, past history of abuse or rape).

5. Spousal abuse (physical, verbal that affects the emotional, etc.).

6. Methods of child discipline (inconsistency, lack of discipline, etc.).

7. Spiritual issues (lack of a spiritual foundation, deterioration of spiritual principles, or opposite or different religious faiths, etc.).

8. Blending of families (former divorce, respect, discipline, decision and leadership issues).

Which of these major factors threaten your marriage? Have you identified them? Is it a financial crisis? Are you a compulsive spender? Are you inconsistent with child discipline? Do you yell or whine when you don't get your way?

Marriage is a Four-Letter Word

During firearms training as a Green Beret in the U.S. Army Special Forces[4], I trained to quickly identify and discriminate between friendly and enemy targets.

The whistle would blow and I would turn 180 degrees and face down range while targets began to pop up from the ground, from behind barricades and from open windows. I would instinctively raise my M4 rifle towards the targets while my mind simultaneously processed data at 1,000 frames a millisecond, racing to determine which targets were threats and which were friendly.

In those fractions of a second, the trigger would be squeezed multiple times sending controlled pairs of 5.56 down range and into the targets eliminating the threats and saving the hostages alive. The overall factor determining which targets were enemy was in the observation of the hands, because hands carry weapons used to kill.

When faced with a threat as a police officer I would raise my firearm and yell, "Show me your HANDS!" "Take your HANDS out of your pockets" "Place your HANDS where I can see them."

Quite often, threats to marriage can be just as simple as the actions of your hands. Do the "hands" of your marriage engage in harmful activities that threaten the marriage?

- Swiping the credit card of debt
- Browsing the web pages of destruction
- Clicking the remote of selfishness
- Ingesting the fruits of addiction
- Engaging the children in poor discipline habits
- Physical and abusive contact during arguments
- Viewing the pleasure of sin for a season
- Throwing objects in frustration
- Punching a wall (yes, it happens).

Chapter 2. Identifying Problems

Marital hands get dirty with issues that threaten the life of their marriage. They are busy. The bad seeds planted will grow into a garden of weeds.

Take a few moments to identify your threats and cleanse your hands and hearts with the water of the Word.[5]

> *"My **hands** also will I lift up unto thy commandments, which I have loved; and I will meditate in thy statutes."*
>
> Psalms 119:48

> *"Draw nigh to God, and he will draw nigh to you. Cleanse your **hands**, ye sinners; and purify your hearts, ye double minded."* James 4:8

Marriage is a Four-Letter Word

Chapter 3

Eliminating Problems

Now that you have learned to identify the real issues within your marriage, and not just symptoms, it's time to begin eliminating them. These five healthy steps will equip you with measurable methods by which to help eliminate those identified issues and increase both effective and productive communication in your marriage. They are:

- Make Communication **Planned**
- Make Communication **Private**
- Make Communication **Productive**
- Make Communication **Positive**
- Make Communication **Prayerful.**

Make it Planned

For important discussions, schedule ahead of time and plan it accordingly. How you go about meaningful conversation makes a difference! If you've never done this before, it could be challenging.

Husband: "*I just checked online and saw how much you spent at the store last night! We need to talk about this right now. What the heck did you buy anyways?*"

This communication method puts the listener on the defense, accusing them of being the problem and demanding an immediate discussion. Plus it is more directive than it is decisive. Is the husband asking his wife to engage in a discussion after dinner or is he demanded to have a discussion? Being disrespectful and/or inconsiderate will most likely lead to a fight.

Discussing finances and excessive spending is important, but how you do it matters most.

Husband: *"Hey babe, how about we sit down and discuss the finances tonight after supper. What do you suggest?"*

See the difference? You're a team. Plan as a team and work as a team.

Last thought: timing is everything. Don't pitch your plan as soon as your spouse walks through the door. Give them some time to unwind.

When it comes to total spoken vocabulary men, in general, have a limit. For example, a man's vocabulary is roughly 15,000 words a day. On the other hand, a woman has an extensive vocabulary of about 60,000 words a day. If compared to the size of this book, men speak two to three chapters a day and women speak nearly the entire book.

A man's vocabulary is running on empty by the time he comes home from work. About the only thing they have on their mind is food and relaxation and, of course sex, if opportunity avails itself.

Men, the problem with this is that the wife still has another 30,000 words to use for the day (half of this book), and she has saved the best conversations for last.....so just as the husband is gearing down for the day, the wife is still on the go.

Even in today's society many wives still spend more time around the house and the conversations they have are primarily by phone, Facebook, Twitter or e-mail. Some have been home with children all day, so they're more than ready for adult conversation (one-on-one) the moment their husband walks through the door.

> **The steps to a prosperous marriage are laid in the building blocks of effective communication. Allow discussions of issues to be planned, private, positive, productive and prayerful so that they can be prosperous.**

Chapter 3. Eliminating Problems

Some spouses are naturally clingy and needy like a puppy. They need affection and confirmations of love when their husband or wife comes home from work. Just like a puppy, if the spouse will hold, pet and play with the puppy for a few moments, it will settle down.

In this analogy, the husband comes home spent from work, but the wife is ready to converse with all the day's activities and dilemmas. The finances. The kids. The dripping faucet. Grandma in the hospital. Aunt Gina's thyroid flair up. Grocery shopping. The long lines. The cookout Friday. The dryer squeak. The *"What do you want for supper?"* The neighbor issue. Johnny's report card. The computer virus. The vacation plan. The wall that Sammy colored…and worst of all – the *"Why don't you talk to me?"* On and on and on. So, what does the husband do? He tunes out and turn off. Is it the right thing for husbands to do? Nope.

Perhaps now you see the communication barriers that some couples face by not understanding each other and not planning meaningful conversation.

Husbands: Realize that you must expand your vocabulary and save your best conversations for your wife. She needs your attention at the end of the day – not the computer, Xbox, or the television. Pay her some meaningful attention when you come home and be less concerned about *you* and more concerned about *her*. Respect the stressors that she has had throughout the day, understanding that you both have various stressors that you deal with differently.

Strive to relieve your wife from some of her stressors. Let her talk to you. Show that you are actively listening. Demonstrate it by putting down the magazine or newspaper. Turn off the TV. Back up from the computer and listen.

Men are *"fixers"* and *"solvers,"* often coming up with solutions to all the issues their wives bring up. Stop! Solutions are not always what they want, men! They just want to talk to you and let things out. They want you to simply shut up, sit down and listen.[1]

Wives: Understand your husband's communication hurdles and approach him positively at the right moment, without overwhelming him with every detail and issue of your life as soon as he walks through the door.

Imagine his day and the stressors that have been placed upon him, some of which he won't talk about. Realize that his home is his castle – his comfort zone away from the hustle and bustle of the workplace (or at least it should be). The last thing he wants to come home to is a war zone.

Therein is the reason why many husbands don't want to come home. They'll spend more time at the office, in a deer stand, a fishing boat, at a buddy's house or the corner bar.[2] It's because a guy doesn't necessarily need the socialization… he needs the peace of relaxation.

Why come home if the dishes and laundry are piled in two mounds and the kids are running around screaming like a tribe of heathens? It's more like a circus than a castle. Why come home if he's going to be bombarded with the 10 major issues of the day as soon as he walks through the door? Work is stress enough…so he doesn't need to face it at home. That's exactly how some men feel.

Now imagine the impact of the stressors when both the husband and wife work 40+ hours a week! Both have heavy workloads, and both have responsibilities when they get home. The work doesn't stop when they walk through the door. The work of home has just begun. If all the energy is placed into work and taking care of the children, automobiles and home….what happens to the intimacy? What happens to meaningful conversations? Therefore, it takes even more *work* in the marriage to make conversations planned and productive, so that problems can be eliminated!

Make it Private

Select a private atmosphere for important discussions. Arrange it for just the two of you. No children. No television. No computers. No phones. No texting.

Choose somewhere with a relaxed atmosphere, free from distractions, interferences and interruptions. A sitting room in your house or a cozy restaurant could be such a place. Although private enough for the two of you,

Chapter 3. Eliminating Problems

it's also public enough so that you are less likely to cause a scene, raise your voice, yell or walk away as you would in the privacy of your home.

Also, choose somewhere your spouse enjoys because they'll be more relaxed, comfortable and willing to discuss issues. Please don't make excuses for not making it private. Always a friend, neighbor or relative can watch your children while you go out. If not, you can always discuss important issues after the children are in bed.

Then there are other alternative events that you can choose, such as a walk in the neighborhood or lunch together at the park. If you want it to be prosperous, make it private.

Whatever the case, do your best to make it free from outside distractions so that you can get down to business.

> **A negative attitude produces negative results, but a positive "can do" attitude produces positive results.**

Timing is everything! Plan your conversations for just the right moment so that you'll achieve the most favorable outcome.

- If you realize that your husband had a bad day at work and you want to talk about his dipping habit – choose a different day!
- If he was just denied a promotion and you need to discuss how much time he spends on the computer – pick a different day.
- If your wife is frustrated with the new shotgun you just bought and you want to discuss finances for the summer vacation – wait!

What you ask, when you ask and how you are learned skills! Children are masters of this trait! Especially that sweet, *innocent* little girl who climbs up on Daddy's lap and looks at him with those big brown eyes, smiles and asks, *"Daddy, can I please have a popsicle?"* She already won his heart before ever asking for the popsicle. *"Sure you can, sweetheart. Anything you want."*

Husbands: Learn this trait. Appeal to your woman's senses and you'll increase your love connection. Your kind comments to her should always precede positive criticism. Make her feel appreciated, loved, attractive and you'll eliminate 99% of the problems in your marriage.

Wives: You generally understand this trait, so use it to your advantage. You know how to feed his ego and use your sex appeal to get what you want. Use it to spice things up and make him feel respected, appreciated, needed and like the king of his castle, with you his queen. Do it because you love, and not just to get what you want. By doing so, you also will eliminate issues.

Make it Positive

Adopt an attitude that facilitates growth and the effective communication of issues. Have a positive mindset that will produce positive results.

If you know that your spouse may avoid you and walk away, decide ahead of time that you're not going to get angry. Instead, force yourself to be positive and in control of your emotions. If you must, look yourself in the mirror and make a commitment to yourself to be upbeat and positive before addressing the issues.

> **With every problem you bring to the table, bring three solutions!**

If you are facing a dilemma that seems to have no prosperous outcome, skip to step five and commit it to prayer. Some issues don't have a positive outcome other than the fact that it will one day be over and nothing more than a memory of the past.

However, on the day-to-day marital issues, you can bring a positive attitude to the discussion table, thus facilitating a productive atmosphere with your spouse.

Make it Productive

"Productive" is the opposite of *"unproductive"* or *"counterproductive,"*

Chapter 3. Eliminating Problems

both of which result in absolutely nothing positive or prosperous. To make communication productive, set clear and reasonable goals for the conversation that include attainable and measurable results.

> *"He that diligently seeketh good procureth favour: but he that seeketh mischief, it shall come unto him."* Proverbs 11:27

I counseled a woman who wanted her husband to quit drinking...and there was no other alternative or compromise. Nice wish, but the husband wasn't going to stop. The more she talked about it, the less he cooperated. The friction had affected all areas of their marriage.

After years of demanding that he stop drinking with no resolve, she came in to talk and I suggested that she find a middle ground with him– one they both could agree upon. She asked him to drink only on the weekends, to which the husband agreed stating that he realized his drinking was interfering with work.

After a few months she was back. "Chaplain, I can't handle it. I want him to quit drinking!" she exclaimed. In finding the middle ground, she asked him to not bring it home, to which he agreed. After a year, her husband quit drinking altogether but it was when he was ready.

His success wasn't through a 12-step program or even the local church. It was through his wife recognizing that her demands were too great for her husband to agree, so she backed off and allowed the small changes to take place over time. Only then did she find the "baby steps" necessary to get her husband pointed in the right direction… and that made the end result productive and promising.

Have alternative solutions that will promote productive progression towards the goal. Before closing the conversation, close the loop with a commitment to each other to cooperate in attaining the end state.

In other words, don't just present the problems, but come up with various solutions and alternatives to the problems.

> ### A display of anger terminates productive communication

A display of anger terminates productive communication. When you feel yourself getting angry (your heart beats faster; your blood pressure rises; you begin breathing faster; your hands begin to clench, etc.), force yourself to remain calm or temporarily step away. Politely request to continue the conversation later.

- Don't just walk away abruptly.
- Don't ignore your spouse either.

> 1. I had a friend who became so angry with his wife that he punched the wall. His fist struck a stud inside the wall and he broke his hand! What a humbling experience it was for him to wear a cast for the next six weeks!
>
> 2. A friend of mine got into an intense argument with his wife. In his fit of anger, he grabbed the television remote control from off the coffee table, walked outside on his balcony and chucked the remote into the apartment complex lake. The next day he was bummed out because he couldn't change the channel on the TV. A new remote from the apartment manager cost him $40!

Communicate that you are getting angry and need to "cool off." It's okay to tell your spouse that you are going to step away, but *WILL* continue the conversation later (tonight, in three hours – be specific).

> *"Honey, I feel myself getting angry about what we are discussing and I don't want to react negatively upon my anger* (to say or do something you will regret). *If I continue, we may end up fighting about it and that's not what I want, so I need to step away so that I can calm down, relax and think clearly about this. Let's talk about it_____(*tonight, in the morning, etc.*). I love you and*

Chapter 3. Eliminating Problems

want to work it out."

If you are on the receiving end of an angered spouse, my advice to you is: Don't fight *fire with fire*. Instead, fight fire with something that will put out the flames. In other words, don't get spun up when your spouse gets spun up. Don't play ball on their court. Don't meet them on their heightened field of battle.

> **The best verbal jujitsu – "A soft answer turneth away wrath: but grievous words stir up anger." Proverbs 15:1**

Have you ever noticed how when you get angry and argue your voice gets louder and your words come faster? Instead of falling into this trap, use a method of talking slower and lower. It's a calming technique known as "verbal judo" – and it's the opposite of the body's response or reaction to anger.

By talking slower, you deliberate your words by thinking about what you are saying, which allows the hearer to see that you are not spun up in the conversation like they are.

By talking lower, you bring calmness to the conversation because you are calmly expressing your thoughts, which enable the hearer to relax and come *down* to your level of reality.

Law enforcement officers are trained in the art of verbal judo and use this technique daily, whether in dealing with a suicidal or homicidal suspect, talking a suspect into a pair of handcuffs, or negotiating a free pizza from the Domino's night shift manager. Negotiation is simple to understand. It's an art that's honed as a child, and transformed into a skill by professionals.

Think about it. When you were a child, you were told, *"Share your toys"* and *"Don't yell at mommy."* You were told, *"Stop your crying and whining," "Be nice to your sister,"* and, *"Don't hit your brother."*

If only married couples would *grow up, share, stop yelling, stop whining, be nice*, and *stop hitting*. Some couples act more like children than they do adults.

Stop arguing and start negotiating. Stop with the unproductive and start with the productive. Incorporate some verbal judo. Deflect the negative and redirect it in another direction. Stop producing more problems and start eliminating them.

Retaliator or Retreater

There are two basic types of reaction to a heated conversation. One is to retaliate and the other is to retreat.

1. **RETALIATE** (dominate). This means to *attack* (to go on the defensive or offensive; to fight back).
2. **RETREAT** (distance). This means to *break contact* (to get away).[3]

A spouse can possess both attributes, but will predominately lean more upon one or the other in the face of adversity.

The RETALIATOR will fight. They'll conduct a verbal assault on their spouse. It won't end well. Everything within a RETALIATOR will want to attack and demand answers as the conversation continues to heat up. They'll follow their spouse around the house demanding to discuss the issues *("I want to talk about this right now!")*. However, RETREATERS are most likely *NOT* to discuss issues the more they are *pushed* by RETALIATORS.

The RETALIATOR often perceive an innocent question as a preemptive strike, such as, *"Did you remember to put gas in the car?"* The RETALIATOR may think that this question is an attack because what they actually hear is, *"You didn't remember to put gas in the car."*

The response will most likely be, *"What? You don't think that I can remember to put gas in the car? Do you think I'm stupid?"*

Often a RETALIATOR will feel like situations are seldom resolved because RETREATERS are generally not very good at expressing themselves…

Chapter 3. Eliminating Problems

whereas RETALIATORS often don't know when to shut up! One says, "You talk too much," and the other says, "You don't talk enough."

Perhaps you are a RETALIATOR. If so, you must train yourself to do what the emotions of the flesh don't want to do – and that's to remain calm, cool and collected. Listen, hear, try to understand and even repeat back what your spouse says.

Never badger, harass or force a conversation with a RETREATER. They will shut you off and tune you out. You may as well talk to the wall because a RETREATER may simply *walk away* rather than face confrontation.

If you are a RETREATER and you don't particularly do well with confrontation, you cannot just walk away and hide your head in the sand, and pretend the conversation didn't happen.[4] You cannot just not talk about it and expect everything to magically work itself out. The RETALIATOR won't likely forget... and the only one you're fooling is yourself. You must face yourself and your spouse by going back to finish the conversation. How you do this will determine the outcome.

A RETALIATOR may be able to *bulldoze* a RETREATER into conforming to your wants, wishes and demands... but if you do, it will only bring satisfaction to you and your side of the relationship. Internally, your spouse won't respect you nor will they be as productive in the relationship as they could be.

Other areas of your marriage will begin to deteriorate besides communication. Quite often, it begins with intimacy in the bedroom. So you must think positive and productive by approaching your spouse from a mindset that places you in their shoes (empathy).

If you are a RETALIATOR, the best thing you can do is realize that you have an extroverted personality trait – a dominant communication style – that may be easily triggered by your spouse. Understand that you have developed in such a way throughout your lifetime. You're a product of your past. It's not a bad thing, it's just an attribute that must be harnessed and used productively. So be considerate and talk with love.

Marriage is a Four-Letter Word

Decide to arrive at a happy medium when discussing issues with your spouse. Find the right time and place to carry out a meaningful, productive discussion. Remain calm and remember to make it both private and positive.

Two RETALIATORS in a marriage makes for a lethal combination because they both want to get the last word. Neither backs down until one overpowers the other and the underdog is crushed by hurled words that strike deep inside the heart. These verbal fights can last for days, weeks and sometimes months. Even when two RETALIATORS *kiss and make up*, they often have a problem forgiving and forgetting (see Chapter 10). Give it a few weeks and they'll begin throwing it up in their spouse's face in the next argument.

> **FACT: verbal aggressiveness often escalates into physical violence.[5]**

On duty as a police officer in 2002, I was called to a domestic disturbance in progress. When I arrived on the scene with my partner, the wife was chasing the husband around the house with a frying pan.[6]

Three neighbors were sitting on the couch in the middle of a poker game, sipping on bottles of 40-ounce malt liquor and watching their two friends fight! For this couple, it was normal! This wasn't the first time we'd had to go out there and separate Juanita and Jarvis. They were both RETALIATORS and had a history of drinking and fighting.

Juanita was short and plump. Jarvis was tall and skinny. Jarvis would get up in her face and run his mouth but Juanita didn't take smack from him. She was a fighter.

Jarvis had a huge lump on his forehead were Juanita had cracked him with an iron skillet. Jarvis was apologetic and stated that he deserved it for the names he called her. Juanita relinquished the frying pan and they both apologized. Neither wished to press charges so we separated the two of them for the evening.

Chapter 3. Eliminating Problems

Juanita and Jarvis had a history of fighting with each other, but they'd always make up. Their relationship certainly wasn't the healthiest, but then again, they had never known what healthy was.

Most couples don't start out like Juanita and Jarvis. Your first date probably wasn't a *smack down* like *WWF*. If it were, you wouldn't have stayed with them very long. Intensive verbal arguments can lead to a shove, a smack or a punch, or worse. The best thing to do to avoid coming to that point is recognize how you react, and choose a healthy method of backing up, backing down, or even retreating.

Two RETREATERS are most likely to stay together long term, some leading successful marriages and some unsuccessful. It depends on how they deal with bitterness and anger that develop on the inside. Without an outlet, much like a valve on a pressure cooker or teakettle, their frustration will only breed contention.

Since RETREATERS are generally unwilling to communicate their problems, mostly due to the disdain of confrontation and contention, the best hope I have for them is to be mentally able to let it go, thereby forgiving and forgetting.

My former Chaplain Assistant[7] (see pic next page) **is Hispanic and we often joke about her dominating personality as a retaliator. Dwan Lerma grew up in El Paso, Texas in a culture that was much different from mine! Dwan recently married and her husband, Miguel, perfectly balances the relationship.**

"Dad usually didn't disciplined us (me and my four brothers), it was Mom! Dad only stepped in when it got out of control, and when Dad stepped in, we knew that we were all in trouble," she told me, "But Mom usually ran the affairs of the home, and Dad went along with it. It's like that with most of my relatives because it's part of our Hispanic culture. The men rarely take charge until they have to. Understanding it and determining to do it God's way helps me respect my husband as the leader of our home."

Marriage is a Four-Letter Word

Many RETREATERS suffer through years of marriage without effectively expressing their true feelings or concerns. They wear plastic faces to hide internal pain. Nobody likes a RETALIATOR'S method of dealing with problems, but at least a RETALIATOR says what they feel. They don't hide it like a RETREATER. Generally, it is the RETREATER that has a greater potential for drifting apart in heart without their partner knowing, because holding their feeling inside makes them a greater candidate for divorce court.

Numerous factors contribute to your style of communication. Your ethnicity plays a major role. Husbands, your style of leadership will be much different if you were raised Filipino, Samoan, German, Puerto Rican or Italian as opposed to *Americano*. Wives, your role in your relationship will be deeply influenced by whether you were raised Canadian, Indonesian, African or Mexican.

Although culture plays a huge role in your character, either partner can take on the role of the RETALIATOR. Plus, you can't use your history as an excuse for your personality. You have the choice to be who you want to be.

- "My dad was abusive and an alcoholic, so that's why I am."
- "I have a short temper because I'm Irish/a redhead."
- "I never amount to anything because I dropped out of school."
- "She's like that because of her mom."
- "Obesity runs in my family, so that's my excuse."

These are nothing more than excuses for people to be and act the way they want. No doubt, that we all have negative influences that mold our character, yet we also have the option to repair unhealthy character or establish new patterns of behavior.

In general, men take the role of the RETREATER because they aren't very good communicators of their feelings, whereas women naturally respond

Chapter 3. Eliminating Problems

based upon their emotions. Men develop the ability to tone out conversations; that is until they've had enough. When they erupt, things are often said and done that leave deep emotional scars.

Eliminate both the RETALIATOR and the RETREATER in your marriage now by identifying it and terminating it. When you see it coming out, stomp it out by forcing yourself to go the opposite direction – the middle ground – a ground where you are neither!

The next and last step in eliminating problems in your marriage will bring you intimately closer to each other and the Lord.

This step breeds unity, and unit breeds success!

Make it Prayerful

The power of a praying couple is limitless. How much more positive could you be than to begin and end the conversation with prayer? God designed and instituted marriage, so who better to get help from in the marriage than God? We, as spouses, need to remember that we are human and humans make mistakes.

> *"For he knoweth our frame; he remembereth that we are dust."*
> Psalm 103:14

Placing God in the middle of your circumstances will make the difference in your love for one another and your willingness to work through issues, despite having the personality of a retaliator or a retreater.

Praying, especially ending the discussion in a clasping of hands and a commitment to do right in the relationship is paramount for a Christian family.

A respected military leader once told me that his wife of 17 years wanted him to be the spiritual leader of the home.

    I said, "That's right. You should be."

Marriage is a Four-Letter Word

He asked, "What can I do to show her that I am?"

I said, "Live it. Prove it by your actions. The next time you discuss an issue, pray with her."

He responded, "Pray with her?"

"Yes." I confirmed. "Pray with her. Your leadership in prayer will show her you care, and confirm that you are trying your best to be the spiritual leader of the home. She'll respond positively towards you and you'll be far more effective at keeping the love alive."

As we close this chapter, I want to encourage you to place God in the center of your marriage. He is the best problem solver and it all begins with a prayer such as this:

"Lord, thank you for our marriage. Forgive us for our shortcomings and help us to forgive each other. We realize that we are two different people with opinions and reactions that are not always compatible. Please help us to work through these issues by communicating effectively.

Allow us to identify problem areas in our marriage and eliminate them with your help. Enable us to draw closer to each other and to you through these issues. Grant us victory to put the past in the past and move forward into our future that you have given us by forgiving and forgetting.

We place you in the middle of our thoughts, our lives, our action and our love. We look to you for wisdom, peace, gentleness and faith towards each other. In Jesus' name, Amen."

By implementing these five P's"....

1. Make Communication **Planned**
2. Make Communication **Private**
3. Make Communication **Productive**
4. Make Communication **Positive**
5. Make Communication **Prayerful**

...you will be **PROSPEROUS** in your outcome.

Chapter 4

Marriage Killers

Mark it down: Storms will come. Some will be showers and some thunderstorms. Some will be accompanied by fierce winds and hail. Some will rip your sail, and some will smash your rudder into pieces. The purpose of this chapter is to make you aware of the dangers because it's the unsuspecting married couples that will be those most overcome by the storms.

Your marriage must withstand the storms of life and remain seaworthy with love, respect and a relationship with the Lord. One of the most dangerous things to do in a marital storm is to tear down your spouse with harsh words known as *verbal killers of the marriage.*

Ever heard of a trigger word? A trigger word or phrase is a topic, phrase or word that emotionally sets someone off. We all know what key words trigger a fight with our spouse (you may hear it referred to as "pushing their button"), but we also know the right words to say to promote love.

Sometimes we purposely push the buttons just to get a reaction or other times to get a laugh. Beware, though. Too much joking crosses over as a lack of appreciation and consideration.

Asking, *"How much time did you put into this meal?"* will produce a negative, retaliating response. Instead, consider commenting, *"Thanks for the time you put into this meal."*

Right now, think about the trigger words or phrases that produce negative responses from your spouse. Can you name a few?

- You **never**_____!
- How come you **always**_____?

- Why don't you **ever**_____?
- Six years ago you_____.
- Before you forget_____.
- Let me remind you again that_____.
- How many times do I have to tell you to_____?

These are the verbal killers of a marriage that need to be identified and eliminated from your marital vocabulary, never to return (Chapters 2 & 3). Part of this process is learning to restructure your questions/comments directed towards your spouse, to produce the most positive results.

For example: instead of asking, "*Why did you spend so much money?*" say, "*Tell me about your purchase.*"

Let's talk about trigger words and phrases.

The D-Word

Of all the damnable words that divide, discourage, demolish and destroy, this is the mother of all marital killers. Once released, this *D-word* can **never** be taken back. It strikes deep into the heart of your spouse causing permanent damage and leaves a wound so infected that no human doctor can treat it.

The *D-word* is DIVORCE.[1]

In premarital counseling, I tell couples to throw this one out of their marital vocabulary and never allow it to surface in the heat of anger. If the *D-word* comes out of your mouth, it's in your heart.

> "... *for out of the abundance of the mouth the heart speaketh.*" Matthew 12:34

If it's in your heart, you've thought about it. If you think on it long enough, then you'll act on it. You bring about what you think about and your actions will always follow your thoughts.[2] Therefore, if you think about divorce, then divorce is what you will eventually get.

Chapter 4. Marriage Killers

> **You bring about what you think about**

Do bank robbers sit around thinking about teaching Sunday school? No. They sit around thinking about robbing banks. Do anglers sit around thinking about facilitating world peace in the Middle East? No. They think about fishing.

- Do you want to be a success? Think success.
- Do you want to be healthy? Think healthy.
- Do you want to be rich? Think rich.
- Do you want to be happy? Think happy.
- Do you want to be encouraged? Think encouragement.[3]

If you want to be a doctor, think about being a doctor. Make it your goal. Consuming thoughts of becoming a doctor will compel you to act and obtain the education you need to graduate with the degrees and certifications to make the contacts, to get the job, to work in the practice and meet the goals that you thought about.

Of course, there may be some setbacks in life and some interference that may rob you of the goal – but the point is you bring to pass what you think about because your actions always follow your thoughts. If you want to be a great husband, wife, father or mother…then make it a consistent thought of your everyday life.

> **In middle school I had a crush on a girl who said she would grow up and become an attorney. 30 years later we reconnected through Facebook. Low and behold, she was an attorney! Her thoughts had propelled her actions, and she brought about what she thought about.[4]**

Marriage is a Four-Letter Word

> **Struggling with foul shots in 8th grade basketball practice at Xenia Christian Academy, Coach Dickens told me, "Brian, I want you to envision the ball going through the hoop. Visualize making the basket. See it. Believe it. Now do it." Coach knew the secret of success – and that is with a little bit of practice, your actions will always follow your thoughts.**[5]

In the book of Luke Chapter 15, verses 11-32, Jesus tells us the story of the *prodigal son*. This younger son left home before he was ready because his heart was set on *"living life in the fast lane."*[6] His actions followed his thoughts and he partied hearty until all his money was wasted and he had nothing left.

He ended up a servant in a foreign country, tending to filthy, unclean pigs. After a while, he *came to his senses* and mentally developed a plan to go back home and seek forgiveness from his father. Yet all the greatest plans in the world are no good unless you act on them. So that's what this young man did. He arose and went back home to dad. His actions followed his thoughts.

> **Negativity is a virus that breeds more negativity!**

It's no mystery that a positive mindset produces positive results and a negative attitude produces negative results. Have you ever noticed how negativity is contagious? Negativity is like a virus. If you spend much time around negative people, chances are that you will become negative. Yet the same is true with positivism. Your *"can do"* attitude will spill over onto others, specifically your spouse and children.

Do you know why marriages experience so much infidelity? It's because one spouse has thought about adultery, which leads to committing the act when the opportunity presented itself. It's the natural downward digression of humankind. Society calls it *"fanaticizing"* and promotes it through magazine, romance novels and prime time television programs such as *Sex in the City* and *Desperate Housewives* – but God calls it sin.

Chapter 4. Marriage Killers

> *"But I say unto you, That whosoever looketh on a woman to lust after her hath committed adultery with her already in his heart."*
> Matthew 5:28

In the book of Joshua chapter seven, a warrior named Achan was an example because of his four acts of disobedience.

1) He saw what wasn't his to take.

2) He coveted it.

3) He took it.

4) He hid it.

In the book of second Samuel chapter 11, King David faltered in the same actions with Bathsheba:

1) He watched her bathe.

2) He lusted after her.

3) He inquired of her.

4) He took her physically and sexually.

5) He ordered her husband Uriah's death.

You can see the downward spiral of both of these men. The sin wasn't in what they saw; it was in what they thought of in their heart. We are faced with temptation all around us that can initiate lust. You can't drive five miles down the freeway without seeing a billboard advertising something lustful. The sin is not in what you see; the sin is in the thoughts associated with what you see. It's not in the first look; it's in the double take.

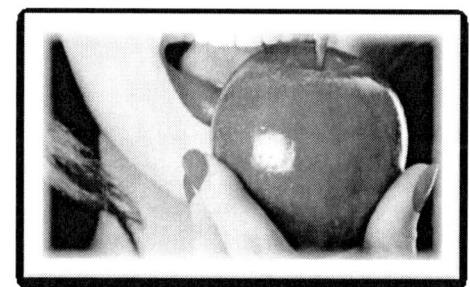

> *"But every man is tempted, when he is drawn away of his own lust, and enticed. Then when lust hath conceived, it bringeth forth sin: and sin, when it is finished, bringeth forth death."* James 1:14-15

Marriage is a Four-Letter Word

> **I shopped for a large flat screen HDTV at Sam's Club. I narrowed my choice down to two favorites and noticed that both boxes containing the televisions were specifically designed with advertisement to entice the buyer. I had to chuckle.**
>
> **One box depicted two professional football players locked together on the line of scrimmage, and the other with a sexy woman posing on a sports car! Why? Advertisers know what attracts men. Next time you shop, look at how items are advertised.[7]**

If you want to have an affair, go ahead and fill your mind with pornography. Think *affair*. Think *infidelity*. It won't be long before opportunity knocks on your door, and you will fall because your thoughts will fuel your actions and propel you to produce what you think about.

The *D-word* is such a problem in marriages that it needs further identification as to why it comes up in the heat of anger.

> **A slip of the tongue is really an expression of the heart**

Have you ever said something that seemed to slip out of your mouth at an awkward time? Perhaps someone has said something like that to you and quickly apologized by stating, *"I'm sorry. I didn't mean to say that."* Ahhhh, but the truth is that you really did mean to say it, or at least you were thinking it, you just didn't want to come right out and say it lest you be embarrassed. The things that *"slip"* out come from the heart and are very real and often true.

Chapter 4. Marriage Killers

> 1. Children are known to blurt out what they are thinking and/or feeling. I remember when my oldest son, Jordan, was a young boy of about four years of age and we paid a visit to my grandmother.
>
> We walked in to greet Grandma and my son plugged his nose and said loudly, "Pheeeewee! Daddy it stinks in here." Needless to say, I was a little embarrassed.
>
> Yes, grandma had that old-person-retirement-home smell, but it's not something you shout aloud! At least Jordan was honest!
>
> 2. Little Johnny was in the back seat of the car and began crying while on the way home from Sunday School. "Johnny, what's wrong? Why are you crying, dear?" said his mother. Young Johnny exclaimed, "The preacher said he wanted us to grow up in a Christian home, but I want to stay with you and dad!

All of these examples are to show you where the *D-word* comes from and why it's important not to think about divorce in your mind. So when you blurt out, *"We should consider a divorce,"* or *"Why don't we just get a divorce already?"* it comes from the heart. Instead of divorce, think of a solution: *"We need to get some marriage counseling!"* or *"We must work through this to be healthy."*

In your marriage, utilize methods of articulating how you feel so that it doesn't result in an argument. Be honest but sensitive. Be wise in your approach by understanding that how and what you say will affect your spouse.

- Just because you think your husband is lazy, doesn't mean you should attack him as such.
- Just because you think your wife can't drive, doesn't mean that you make fun of her.
- Just because she doesn't flatter the dress, doesn't mean that you should degrade her.
- Just because he didn't finish college, doesn't mean you have to put him down.
- Just because he's irresponsible with finances, doesn't mean you tell him he's an idiot.

Marriage is a Four-Letter Word

- Just because you're insecure, doesn't mean that you have to accuse them of cheating with someone on *Facebook*.
- Just because he's not *Bob the Builder*, doesn't mean you have to compare him with your dad.

There are ways to get the point across with love, respect and appreciation. You don't have to fight and argue about it.

───────────

By now, you see how the heart plays a tremendous part in what we say. If you bring up divorce, it's because you have allowed yourself to be influenced by its thoughts. The slip of the tongue is really an expression of the heart.

When you go through a valley in your marriage, avoid thinking about divorce or separation. Avoid the negative and reaffirm the positive by firmly stating, *"We are going to work though this and get the help we need!"*

If you have brought up the *D-word*, there's still hope. Simply ask forgiveness from the Lord, from your spouse – and forgive yourself. Put away the negative thoughts and surround yourself with positive couples who are happily married and in it for the long haul!

Hate

"Hate the player, not the game," "Don't be a hater" and *"Haters gonna' hate"* are familiar phrases that teenagers are using nowadays. They are contradictory statements that really don't make a lot of sense in the context used, but arguably influential in deflecting and redirecting anger.

In life, there are some things to hate such as abuse, rape, murder, drugs, lies, frauds, and infidelity in a marriage. You can come up with your own list.

In God's Word - the Holy Bible – there are some things that He expects us to hate:

> *"Hate the evil, and love the good…"* Amos 5:15
>
> *"Ye that love the LORD, hate evil:"* Psalms 97:10

King David stated,

- *"I will set no wicked thing before mine eyes: I hate the work of them that turn aside; it shall not cleave to me."* Psalms 101:3
- *"Through thy precepts I get understanding: therefore I hate every false way."* Psalms 119:104
- *"I hate vain thoughts: but thy law do I love."* Psalms 119:113
- *"Therefore I esteem all thy precepts concerning all things to be right; and I hate every false way."* Psalms 119:128
- *"I hate and abhor lying: but thy law do I love."* Psalms 119:163

King Solomon stated,

- *"These six things doth the LORD hate: yea, seven are an abomination unto him: A proud look, a lying tongue, and hands that shed innocent blood, An heart that deviseth wicked imaginations, feet that be swift in running to mischief, A false witness that speaketh lies, and he that soweth discord among brethren."* Proverbs 6:16-19
- *"A time to love, and a time to hate; a time of war, and a time of peace."* Ecclesiastes 3:8

We are to hate wrongdoing, but love righteousness. Hate sin, but love the sinner. Hate divorce. Hate separation. Hate negativity. Hate lies. Hate abuse. Hate what sin does to relationships without being a hater of people. Jesus Christ was the greatest example of this type of balance.[8]

Don't go to bed angry

Anger is different to hatred. We can be angry without hating and we can hate without being angry, but when the two merge, it forms a violent concoction. Therefore, when your hatred is directed towards your spouse, *hate* becomes the second degrading characteristic that should be removed from your marital vocabulary.

> *"Be ye angry, and sin not: let not the sun go down upon your wrath:"* Ephesians 4:26

Marriage is a Four-Letter Word

This verse is packed with marital vitamins and minerals. Being angry for the right reason is acceptable when your anger is controlled. So she wrecked the car because she was talking on her cell phone, applying lipstick and backing up at the same time. Be angry – but sin not. So he missed dinner and was too incompetent to call. Be angry – but sin not.

How you express your anger makes the difference. Say that you're angry. Tell them. Let it out, but don't scream it out and don't fight it out. There's no need to raise your voice or be hateful.

Your spouse will be able to tell by your body language that you are angry.

The second part of the verse is summed up as, *"Don't go to bed angry."* Talk it out. Work it out. Make up and then make out.

In schools, churches and homes, we teach our children not say, *"Hate"* because we know they develop a tendency to say it. You've heard them say, *"I hate you"* when they get mad at their sister, or *"I hate school,"* or *"I hate vegetables,"* when they don't like to eat them.

> **While deployed, my wife told me that she had to wash Izak's mouth out with soap. Wow. I was stunned. Is that still done in America? He probably deserved it, but I couldn't imagine my wife going to these measures.**
>
> **Little did I understand how fed-up she was with Izak saying, "I hate this," and "I hate that" (school, vegetables, chores, etc.). Apparently, Izak's encounter with a bar of soap quickly modified his behavior. According to Tracy, Izak hasn't hated anything recently. It's a miracle.**

What would modify your behavior? Would it take a bar of soap? We discipline and admonish our own children, but why not follow the same rules as adults?

It's never beneficial to yell at your spouse, *"I hate you"* or *"I hate it when you _____."* Once those hateful words are out, you'll never get them back.

Just like a teenager angry with their parents; they stomp down the hall, slam the door and yell, *"I hate you!"* If you've ever done that, you know exactly what I'm saying.

Name Calling

It's sad that I have to bring this up, but married adults sometimes act like the biggest babies! Remember this statement from childhood: *"Sticks and stones may break my bones but words will never hurt me?"*

What good has name-calling ever done? Does it have a benefit in the marriage? The only benefit is a selfish one in that it temporarily satisfies the one throwing the names around, but does absolutely nothing to facilitate healthy communication.

Name-calling is childish, selfish and immature. It shows poor character, lack of self-control and articulation, and the inability to communicate effectively.

You would think that the majority of couples slinging names back and forth are young, newly married couples. However, this type of behavior crosses all boundaries of marriage. I've counseled couples who have been married for eight to ten years who still carry on like two six-year-olds fighting over a Barbie doll.

Couples that find themselves at this low level of miscommunication have to work hard to pull out and grow out of it. Name-calling is a way of expressing how you feel, and it's usually accompanied by a flurry of colorless profane metaphors. Consistent name-calling is psychological abuse, especially when accompanied by profanity and degrading remarks.

Put-Downs

"You're never going to amount to anything."

Marriage is a Four-Letter Word

"Can't you do anything right?"

"You're an idiot!"

"Why do you always screw things up?"

"You need to go back to school and get an education."

"Didn't your mother teach you anything?"

"You don't benefit this family at all."

"You're useless to this family."

"Why can't you ever balance the checkbook?"

"A real father would do _____."

"If you weren't so _____, you'd be able to do this."

"Why can't you be like your brother/sister?"

"Quit being such a _____." "You're about as dumb as _____."

"If you were a real _____…"

"If you weren't such a _____, you could _____."

"You always _____."

"You never _____."

These examples of verbal assaults destroy, subtract and divide relationships. They do nothing to build, enhance or reinforce character in your spouse or your children. Each time you direct derogatory statements towards another person, you are inadvertently proclaiming your own self-worth.

> *"Most men will proclaim every one his own goodness: but a faithful man who can find?"* Proverbs 20:6

Making a statement such as, *"You're never going to amount to anything"* sends a clear message to the receiver that you think, "I'm somebody." Are you really better than they are? Saying, *"You're useless to this family,"* makes the statement that you are useful to the family, but they are not. Imagine what these statements do to the self-esteem of a child or teenager!

Chapter 4. Marriage Killers

> **Never discourage anyone who is making progress – no matter how slow the progress**

Often times it's the abuser that suffers from low confidence and self-esteem… therefore they take their frustrations out on others. Perhaps you were the victim of a micromanaging, psychologically damaging spouse, parent or guardian who always told you that you were no good. Those that are victims of this type of behavior often act in a defensive manner, and usually are more guarded in their everyday interactions with people. They were hurt in the past and, without thinking, they remain guarded so as not to be hurt again.

It's unfortunate that they may also carry forth the same traits if not identified and eliminated from their character. Words, comments, and especially the feelings won't ever be erased from a verbally battered spouse or child. Talking down to your spouse is destructive behavior that will end your marriage in divorce. Never talk down to – but instead, build up. Encourage. Compliment. Develop. Love.

Profanity

Profanity can also be pornography – which is a major contributor to killing marriages. However, this section is not about porn, but about the mouth. It's amazing how many people can't complete a sentence without cursing. It takes a higher level of personal character **NOT** to use profanity in your language. Why? It's easy to curse. Duh. It requires no brains. There's no thought process behind it. But to replace those curse words with descriptive adjectives, verbs and adverbs… now that takes character!

> I get apologies all the time…"Sorry Chaplain. I didn't mean to say that," and I think, "Yes you did. You just didn't mean to say it in front of me!" "Please excuse my French." French? I'm certain that was English. "Sorry about that preacher." I respond, "Don't tell me, tell Him," and point up to Heaven.

Marriage is a Four-Letter Word

When you use profanity, you are showing how unthoughtful, uncontrolled and unprofessional you really are. It's a habit that's more addictive than nicotine or alcohol and it's a tough habit to break! You may quit smoking but try to quit cursing and see how long it takes. The flesh picks up those words and doesn't want to let go easily…..and just as soon as you think you have the victory, something or someone will get under your skin and you'll be tested.

Admittedly, your environment contributes to your vocabulary. Therefore, if your work environment is full of profanity, it won't be long before you begin to go down that same verbal path. That is, unless you safeguard your mouth and bridle your tongue.

What is interesting to me it that some people curse at work but don't curse at home. It's as if they flip a switch. They'll tell a dirty joke or use profanity at work because it's acceptable, but clean up their language at home because it's unacceptable around the children. They act a certain way and say things at work that they'd never say around their family, parents or the pastor. I witness this almost daily in the military. Soldiers and leaders put on a uniform, and they put on a language and attitude that goes with the uniform. It's hypocrisy.

Some men experience a lack of control at work - perhaps they're not the leader they want to be or they don't have the position they think they should have - so when they come home they *rule-the-roost* by being over-possessive, obsessive, demanding and manipulative.

Some spouses, however, bring work home with them and treat their family no different from their employees or co-workers. They talk down to their spouse the same way they talk to their buddies or employees at the job site… and see nothing wrong with their behavior! Those type of actions destroy marriages!

If you act a certain way and use a different vocabulary at work, at church, or with your friends than you do at home, you are living a double-standard life.

> *"A double minded man is unstable in all his ways."* James 1:8

If you are in a leadership position at work that requires firmness, that doesn't mean that you can't possess and exhibit self-discipline and character

Chapter 4. Marriage Killers

traits of love, joy, peace, longsuffering, gentleness, goodness, faith, meekness and temperance. You can be assertive and firm as a CEO, Cop, Commando, or Command Sergeant Major without ever living a double-standard life.

> **From 2003 to 2005, I served as the Senior Drill Instructor over a platoon of other Drill Sergeants. Throughout Drill Sergeant School and in all my interactions with infantrymen Soldiers, I never used profanity. Not once.**
>
> **That doesn't mean I was soft on Soldiers – it means that I was most professional. They still feared and respected me – indeed much more so because I got my point across without filling space with meaningless jargon and colorless metaphors. It can be done!**

Here's what's odd - although men are the largest violators of consistent profanity, it's becoming more and more common to hear women spew forth profanity. It's alarming. Makes you scratch your head in wonderment like watching a woman spit chewing tobacco, run a jackhammer or pastor a church congregation! Yes, it's becoming acceptable in society but it's still odd.

Historically, women have been softer, kinder and gentler. When a woman entered the room, men would stand out of courtesy. Fathers taught their sons to open the car door for a woman, or pull out their chair for them and men would apologize for using profanity around women.

Yet today, women are just as bad as men are when it comes to using profanity. Some are worse – like the woman I heard the other day dropping the *f-bomb* multiple time. Is there no more shame in America? Can you remember the last time you saw a woman blush?[9] The morality of America is crumbling faster than the rate of divorce, and the God we use to trust in (*"In God We Trust"*) is shaking his head in disgust.

Besides the work environment, the largest proponent by which our private

Marriage is a Four-Letter Word

lives are invaded by profanity is through media! Television programs, movies and video games provide enough cursing to fill any person's vocabulary. No matter where you turn, it seems like you can't get away from it.

> **Several years ago, I bought a special Sanyo DVD player at Wal-Mart. It's not just any ol' DVD player... it has a built-in language filter that edits out profanity.**
>
> **I brought it home, set it up and watched Blackhawk Down, a war movie based on the historical battle with U.S. Army Rangers and Delta Operatives in Mogadishu, Somalia.[10] There was so much profanity in the movie that I missed half of the dialogue because every other word was filtered out.**

It would be wise for couples to make good choices for the influences they subject themselves. Profanity has no place in the home, and definitely no place when directed towards each other. If you do have a habit of cursing, ask yourself, *"Why? Why do I curse?"* What good does it do you? Does it make you feel more macho or accepted? Do you blame it on the people around you or your environment?

- "I curse because everyone else does."
- "That's the way it is in my office."
- "If only she hadn't done that to make me mad…"
- "If he would've done it differently…"
- "I'm like this because I'm Irish."
- "It's the military!"

Bad habits can be broken, so why not put forth maximum effort to stop? Instead of allowing *"things"* and *"stressors"* to influence and control you, why not control them? You don't need a special program to stop cursing. You need the one book that will conform and transform your thinking. It's not a self-help book from *Barnes & Noble*. You'll have trouble finding the right one at *Borders Bookstore*. It's the most hated, the most loved, the most sold and the most stolen book in all the world.[11] And if you help yourself to it, it will change your life. It's called the Bible.

Chapter 4. Marriage Killers

> *"Create in me a clean heart, O God; and renew a right spirit within me."* Psalm 51:10

As mentioned earlier, when you express the *D-word*, the words that are in your heart come out your mouth.[12] So to clean up your mouth from cursing, you gotta' clean out your heart! Change comes from within and works its way to the outside.[13]

Cursing often accompanies name-calling and put-downs. These types of arguments become intense with nothing positive accomplished. It shows your frustration, lack of control and anger.

Profanity has no place in your marriage. When directed towards your spouse, it chips away at the marital foundation, little by little, until it crumbles. It takes the power of God to mortify the flesh, bridle the tongue and transform the heart to eliminate those words from the vocabulary.

> *"But now ye also put off all these; anger, wrath, malice, blasphemy, **filthy communication** out of your mouth."* Colossians 3:8

> *"Let no **corrupt communication** proceed out of your mouth, but that which is good to the use of edifying, that it may minister grace unto the hearers."* Ephesians 4:29

> *"For the sin of their mouth and the **words of their lips** let them even be taken in their pride: and for **cursing and lying** which they speak."* Psalms 59:12

> *Let your **speech** be alway with grace, seasoned with salt, that ye may know how ye ought to answer every man."* Colossians 4:6

> *"Let the **words of my mouth**, and the meditation of my heart, be acceptable in thy sight, O LORD, my strength, and my redeemer."* Psalms 19:14

The *D-word*, hate, name-calling, put-downs and using profanity – these are the top killers of a marriage. They're all intertwined like a knitted garment with a dark stain that can't be easily removed. Change your marriage by terminating these verbal killers, and by allowing God to work in your heart.

Marriage is a Four-Letter Word

Chapter 5

Start Right, Stay Right, Finish Right

Marriage takes work, and, more specifically, it takes keeping the love alive. There's a thought I would like to bring out that contributes to long-term, lifetime marital success. It comes from my mentor Dr. Greg Estep who said it best...[1]

"If you start right and stay right – you'll finish right."

Many couples don't start right. They start with the wrong intentions from the very beginning. The right intentions are to look for marriage material – the characteristics and qualities in the life of a person you would like to marry; not to look to "hook-up."

Yet after *hooking up* and becoming an item (committing to each other in whatever way they choose), many couples fail to abide by a simple guideline established by God, which is to abstain from fornication.[2] For guys, let me break it down in football terms. This phase of *"hooking up"* is called the *kickoff*.

After the *kickoff*, one thing leads to another and eventually they move in together. I call this the *pre-season*. Sometimes children are produced during the *kickoff* and *pre-season* and they grow up without a parent.

The couples are not married; they're unsure about getting married (the *full season*); they haven't undergone premarital counseling (*coaching & training*); they don't have God in their relationship (*contract*), nor do they have a personal relationship with Him (*ownership*) – at least not one strong enough to start right.

> **"Drive-Through Weddings are offered at a Florida Store for $20."**
> **Fox News**[3]

Marriage is a Four-Letter Word

Their excuse for living together is to determine if they are *compatible* – which is society's worldly philosophy for determining whether the relationship will work out between them. They have already developed a *renter's* mentality towards the relationship instead of an *owner's* mentality.[4]

The percentage of couples that actually make it to the marital altar are now choosing more unconventional methods of *tying the knot*. I call these methods *"drive-thru weddings"* of convenience.[5]

- They run off to the Justice of the Peace.
- They pick a clergy from the phone book by using the *"Eeny Meeny Miny Mo"* method.
- They get married online. A new and popular method that's also called, *"Marriage by Mail."*[6]
- They'll claim "common-law" marriage after X amount of years.[7]
- Or they'll use a variety of other methods to make it *official* according to their state laws.

So off they go on a lifelong, life commitment adventure expecting everything to work out magically.

Can it work out from here? Yes. But it will take a whole lotta' work and great resiliency to endure the reaping process of the *"false start,"* the *"delay of game"* and the *"illegal procedure."*

A marriage that started wrong will face much unexpected and unnecessary hardship in the years ahead. It's difficult to fix what you know is broken but don't understand why. It's easier to toss what is broken to the curb and start anew... but that's the coward's way out.

> **"What goes around, comes around" is a famous quote based on the Biblical laws of sowing and reaping**

Have you ever heard the term, *"You reap what you sow"* or *"What goes around comes around?"* Both terms mean essentially the same thing, and they came from the pages of history about 1950 years ago. Here it is...

*"Be not deceived; God is not mocked: for **whatsoever a man***

Chapter 5. Start Right, Stay Right, Finish Right

soweth, that shall he also reap. For he that soweth to his flesh shall of the flesh reap corruption; but he that soweth to the Spirit shall of the Spirit reap life everlasting." Galatians 6:7-8

The list of seeds that reap a bad crop are given in preceding verses and, ironically, the first two are sexual sins.

"Now the works of the flesh are manifest, which are these; **Adultery, fornication**, *uncleanness, lasciviousness, idolatry, witchcraft, hatred, variance, emulations, wrath, strife, seditions, heresies, envyings, murders, drunkenness, revellings, and such like..."*
Galatians 5:19-21

The average couple that comes to me for counseling did not start right. They're experiencing the abnormal share of issues, and they expect me to fix their marriage like a mechanic changes a tire. It just isn't that simple. It's the equivalent of attempting to rescue a runaway train, at full-speed, that is off its tracks. It's nearly impossible to get it back on track.

"But Jesus beheld them, and said unto them, With men this is impossible; but with God all things are possible."
Matthew 19:16-26

There is no overnight quick fix. If there were, the divorce rate wouldn't be at 51%. The key to getting things right in a marriage is to build or rebuild the foundation on rock instead of shifting sand.[8] It requires educating the couple on what a proper marriage is, what it looks like, who's in charge of it, how it works together, and who should be in the center of it. Had it started right, it would have had a better chance of staying right so that it can finish right.

Dr. Estep often used the **Laws of Sowing and Reaping** in relation to life choices:

1. You reap **WHAT** you sow.

2. You reap **LATER** than you sow.

3. You reap **MORE** than you sow.

Dr. Peter S. Ruckman, President of Pensacola Bible Institute, has a footnote in his reference Bible next to Galatians 6:7.[9] In addition to the points that Dr, Estep uses, Ruckman adds, *"You reap according to how you sow (2 Cor.*

9:6)."

> *"But this I say, He which soweth sparingly shall reap also sparingly; and he which soweth bountifully shall reap also bountifully."*
> 2 Corinthians 9:6

Let's unite and discuss these laws of sowing and reaping in four main points that will explain many of the issues that occur in our personal life, as well as our marriage.

1. You reap **WHAT** you sow.

2. You reap **LATER** than you sow.

3. You reap **MORE** than you sow.

4. You reap according to **HOW** you sow.

Law #1: You reap WHAT you sow

If you plant bad crops (corruption), you'll reap bad crops (corruption). If you plant good crops, you'll reap good crops. You can't do wrong and reap right nor can you do right and reap wrong.

You may be asking, *"Then why do I reap good and bad?"* Ah-ha! Good question. The reason is simple. Some people go throughout their lifetime like they're on the Rock 'n' Roller Coaster at Walt Disney World in Orlando, Florida –up and down, up and down, tossed around at full speed. One day is good and the next day is bad; one day a curse and the next day a blessing. One day on a high and the next day on a low.

The fact of the matter is, each day we plant both good and bad seed. Both crops have the potential to spring up – sometimes one right after another and sometimes at the same time.

The *Laws of Sowing and Reaping* apply to all people whether saved (born again) or lost; with or without Christ in their heart.[10] We all reap what we plant. Say it aloud with me: We all reap what we sow.

Chapter 5. Start Right, Stay Right, Finish Right

> **As a young boy of 12 or 13 years of age, I got in trouble for shooting at the neighbor's Christmas lights with my BB gun. Hiding a smile on his face, Dad took away my rifle and warned me not to do that again. Later I learned that Dad, when he was a teen, had his BB gun taken away for the same reason!**

For those with grown children, did they ever get in trouble by doing something similar to what you did as a teenager? Sure they did! Have you ever heard someone say, *"I hope my kid doesn't turn out half as bad as I was?"* The troublesome fact is that they probably will!

- Have you ever been lied to?
- Have you ever had someone hold open a door for you?
- Have you ever had someone buy you lunch?
- Have you ever received a dent in your car door at the supermarket?
- Have you ever had someone curse you out when you cut them off in traffic?
- Have you ever had someone treat you to an unexpected blessing?

If you can identify with these examples, it's probably because you did the same thing to/for someone else at some time in your past. You see, reaping comes in different forms and through different means. But, overall, pound for pound, tit for tat, you still reap what you sow.

If you started your marital relationship out wrong, as many couples do, you'll reap the fruit of it. It may be a constant string of arguing and fighting; it may be an unplanned birth; it may be financial disaster; it may be some type of health issue; it may end in divorce, or it may be some other form of corruption that the Lord allows.

If you continue the pattern without acceptance and repentance, you'll continue to reap negatively.

Marriage is a Four-Letter Word

Law #2: *You reap LATER than you sow*

The negative seeds of sin you plant won't necessarily spring up and produce fruit tomorrow. They take time. It may be years down the road, and unless God grants you mercy, you will reap a bad crop later.

> On a cold January morning in 2002, I left the house to go to work and as I walked to my car (which was parked on the street in front of the house) I noticed a huge dent in the driver's door; a crease all the way from the top to the bottom.
>
> I stood there in disbelief for a moment, and then attempted to pry it open. The door creaked and moaned as I tugged on it, finally opening enough for me to slide inside. I started the engine, but my internal engine was already cranked and I wondered how it had happened.
>
> I got out and tried to slam the door shut but barely got it to latch. As I stood there pondering, I began to investigate the scene of this unjust atrocity. I noticed tire tracks in the snow. They came from my neighbor's driveway and directly into my car, and then off down the road.
>
> I remembered hearing a party there last night, so as I scanned my eyes to my neighbor's house, I saw more clues – beer bottles scattered in the snow. I remembered cars parked up and down the block, so I calculated that some drunken idiot from the party had backed out of my neighbor's driveway, smashed my car door with his rear bumper, and sped off down the street.
>
> With vehement determination, I marched up to my neighbor's door

and beat on it as if I was serving a search warrant. I had my police uniform on and thought for sure I'd be able to get the truth out of him. Finally, Joe "the Pothead" (yes, my neighbor) came to the door wiping the sleep out of his eyes and squinting in the morning light.

"Look, man," I said, "One of your buddies took off out of your driveway last night and hit my car. That's a hit and run! I'm not too happy about it, and if I find out who did it, they're not going to be very happy about it either. What's the deal?"

"Aw dude. Man, I uhhhh, I dunno who did it. Man, are you sure about it?" He said.

"Yeah I'm sure! Look at the tire tracks!" I exclaimed and directed his attention to the tracks in the snow. "Look at my car!"

"Well, dude… I didn't see anything. Sorry man," he replied.

"Yeah, I figured you didn't," I said, and marched away mumbling under my breath. As I got in my car and drove away, I calculated the costs of repairs in my mind, "The car is paid off," I said, "I only have liability insurance. Shoot! Repairs and paint will probably cost me $1,500!"

"God, I don't need this," I said. "Lord, I'm trying to do right, live right, and serve you." I began bargaining with God. "Father, I don't have the money to fix this, nor is it worth it. Now I have to drive around in a car with a big dent in the door! What did I do to deserve this?"

All of a sudden, out of nowhere, God tapped on my heart and replied, "What about the cars that you hit and ran on?"

"God," I replied, "That was years ago when I was a teenager. And some of them, well, I take that back, most of them were accidents, you know…"

"Some of them," God said, "But you still reap what you sow." And to that, I could do nothing but remain silent for the rest of the trip to work, listening and feeling the cold air stream in from the gap between my door and the window frame.

Marriage is a Four-Letter Word

You see, we reap what we sow, and it comes later and it's always more than we planted, based on our heart's motive. This law carries over into every area of life.

Law #3: *You reap MORE than you sow*

So often we equate the *Laws of Sowing and Reaping* to only the *"bad stuff"* that happens to us. The verse states, *"For he that soweth to his flesh shall of the flesh reap corruption..."*[11] The context shows us that corruption can be reaped in different forms, but it's still all corruption!

> **When Tracy and I planted our first garden, what a chore it was! Something I thought would be so easy became a daily battle to reap a decent crop. We tilled, we planted, we weeded, we watered. Oddly enough, I reaped tomatoes where I planted lettuce, and I reaped carrots in rows of tomatoes and peppers! I swore that I didn't plant carrots in rows of tomatoes, but somehow I reaped them. On top of it all, I waged a war on weeds and was miserably defeated!**

I recall an example from Tom Gresham, the Chaplain Director of Religious Services for the Green County Adult Detention Center in Xenia, Ohio.[12]

In counseling inmates who claimed to be *innocent* of the crimes against them, Gresham made good use of the word *corruption* to explain the law of sowing and reaping as found in Galatians chapter six:

> Inmate: "*Man, I don't deserve to be in here! I'm innocent!*"

> Chaplain Gresham: "So you didn't do the crime?"

> Inmate: "*Naw man. I didn't do what they locked me up in here fo'. I ain't no gun slinger. I was just rollin' with my homies when the Po-Po done swooped down on me. They got me in here for gun charges man... but it wasn't even mine! My home boy put it under the seat when they flipped the strobes on us!*"

Chapter 5. Start Right, Stay Right, Finish Right

Chaplain Gresham: "Wow! That's pretty corrupt, don't you think?"

Inmate: *"Yeah, man. That's messed up. They be playin' me like I'm sum chump up in here. They be some corrupt cops!"*

Chaplain Gresham would open his King James Bible to Galatians 6:7-8 and read, *"Be not deceived; God is not mocked: for whatsoever a man soweth, that shall he also reap.* **For he that soweth to his flesh shall of the flesh reap corruption;** *but he that soweth to the Spirit shall of the spirit reap life everlasting."*

Chaplain Gresham: "What's this verse say right here?" as he pointed to the verse, "*He that soweth to his flesh shall of the flesh reap….*"

Chaplain Gresham: "What's the next word?"

Inmate: "Corruption."

Chaplain Gresham: "That's right. Corruption is dishonest or illegal behavior. You're reaping corruption. You may not have put the gun under the seat, you're reaping what you planted, and it's all corrupt. Think about all the things you've done in the past that you never were caught for? How many times should you have been busted by the police, but never were? How many times should you have ended up with silver bracelets, dragged down town and thrown in here?"

Inmate: "Yeah, you're right. I see your point."

> **"The key to a successful garden is using good soil as the foundation"**
> *~ Brigadier General Willard M. Burleson III*[13]

Consider your own life. How has this law had an effect on you? Ever heard the saying, *"When it rains it pours?"* When you reap negativity in your marriage, it may not be the exact negative seed that you planted… but it will still be a corrupt crop of some sort.

I've had money, electronics, gear, tools and car stereos stolen. I've been

Marriage is a Four-Letter Word

cheated, talked about, lied to, cussed out, flipped off, kicked out, cut off and run out. I have reaped my share of corruption. Don't get me wrong – I have a blessed life and God is good, but I've deservingly reaped my share of bad crops.

The balance between what I've planted and what I've reaped sometimes seems unfair, but the crops are always more than the seeds. The truth of the matter is, if I had gotten what I deserved, I should be in hell with my back broken. God has been merciful to me a sinner. If you're honest, you'll feel the same way!

Let me tell you how blessed I am.

Over the years, I've been given money, TVs, furniture, tickets, groceries, a truck and two cars. I've been given jobs, opportunities, friendships, relationships, kindness and blessings beyond compare. I've been promoted, awarded, nominated, recognized and complimented more times than I can remember.

I've served as a Green Beret, trained hundreds of Soldiers, filmed for television, climbed the tallest mountains in Austria, jumped with the Golden Knights, kissed the road to Rome, and skied treacherous mountains of Kosovo.

I was given a monkey by a jungle tribe, wrestled a bear, fought a killer K-9, and swam with sharks.[14] I've fought against guns, knives, needles and a chainsaw.[15] I've been peppered sprayed, tasered, shocked, stabbed, burned, punched, kicked, run over, mortared and shot at.

I've been in five car crashes, numerous motorcycle, dirt bike and ATV wrecks, had seven parachute tree landings and survived a blizzard at on Mt. Rainier! Fifteen times I've had stitches, staples or a metal plate in my body! Multiple times I should've died and often times wonder why God spared me.

I've survived war in the middle east, experienced the waterfalls in the Philippines, stood before the Pyramids of Egypt, savored the sunrise on the beaches in Spain, navigated volcanic glaciers in Iceland, bathed in mountain streams in Mexico, experienced Hungary from a hot air balloon,

Chapter 5. Start Right, Stay Right, Finish Right

dined with the King of Kuwait, and presented with an award by the President of Serbia.[16]

I've preached at weddings, funerals, churches; conducted conferences and seminars to small groups and packed-out crowds. I've seen hundreds come to salvation in Jesus Christ, salvaged numerous marriages, performed countless weddings, and trained hundreds of couples to reach the finish line.

I've viewed ocean sunsets in the arms of my wonderful wife and experienced the overwhelming joy of three healthy, beautiful boys take their first breath and open pure, blue eyes to a brand new world.

Mt. Rainer, WA

I have reaped such great crops from the good seeds I have planted, that many times they overshadow the bad crops that come up. I'm a nobody... a nobody that God blesses.

So in your marriage, be encouraged to sow those good seeds daily. In time....you'll reap them.

Law #4: You reap according to HOW you sow

Here are the facts:

- The more good you plant, the more good you'll reap.
- The more corruption you plant, the more corruption you'll reap.

We understand that. Now we must consider an element that's not been previously stated:

> *"...for man looketh on the outward appearance, but the LORD looketh on the heart."* 1 Samuel 17:6

Man is not to be the judge of motives... God is.[17] He not only sees what we do but He knows why we do it!

Have you ever done something stupid and said, *"I can't believe I just did that?"* Perhaps we don't understand why we do some of the things we do (besides living in a sin-cursed body on a sin-cursed earth) – but God understands.

Nothing we do or say escapes Him. He's Omniscient. Therefore, if you are bent on doing wrong in the relationship, God sees it and you'll reap proportionally according to your heart.

For those of you that have read the historical event of King David and Bathsheba, did you ever wonder why God was merciful to David? After all, he was an adulterer and murderer. What if your President was an adulterer and a murderer? Would you vote for him next term?

Why did God consider Lot righteous when, after all, he ended up in a cave having sex with his two daughters (2 Peter 2:7)? What about Rahab the harlot or the woman Jesus spoke to at the well that had been divorced five times? Why is it that Peter is standing up and leading over 3,000 new believers after denying the Lord three times?

These epic examples of God's mercy and grace show us that He (unlike us) looks past man's futile reasoning and sees the heart's motive. In fact, Jesus Christ even read people's minds and answered their thoughts![18]

God knows your heart. If it's bent on doing wrong… you'll reap proportionally more than if you mess up and confess up with a repetitive and contrite heart that cries out for God's forgiveness.

We Didn't Start Right. Now What?

Thankfully, with God all things are possible, so if you have fallen into the statistic category, don't give up! There's still hope, but hope isn't found in dope (any mind-altering chemical, pill or alcohol), a rope (suicide) or the pope (religion).[19]

> **Marriage is not 50/50. It's 100/100**

Chapter 5. Start Right, Stay Right, Finish Right

Your problems won't miraculously solve themselves if you incorporate the philosophies of Dr. Phil, Dr. Oz, Dr. Seuss, or Dr. Spock. Although highly recommended, 40 days of The Love Dare from the movie Fireproof doesn't work for everyone.[20] Oprah and Jerry Springer can't give you what you need. Turning over a new leaf or making a new year's resolution won't set your runaway train back on the tracks. Understanding your spouse's love language will help – but it's still not the ultimate fix to an ultimate mess.[21] And one-sided commitment to change only goes so far because marriage is not 50/50…it's 100/100.

If you've come to the point where it seems like you've tried everything and nothing works… why not try something that's out of this world? Why not try Christ? Repair for your marriage, through divorce, and into your future relationship will require a radical transformation and unwavering commitment to the Lord, and each other. Remember, internal issues can't be fixed with external methods. Both sides must be willing to work together externally while getting the help and resources they need internally.

> **Take a pig out of his muddy pen. Bathe him. Scrub him. Clean him up. Dry him. Brush him. Dress him. Feed him. Talk to him and tell him that he's no longer a pig. Now let him go. Where does he run? Why? He's a pig. You can't change the external without changing the internal.**

Since your marriage must be transformed from the inside out, begin first by seeking out a Godly counselor and/or pastor to work through the issues with your spouse. Accept and place God between you and your circumstances, relying on Him as your firm foundation. Everything else is shifting, sinking sand.

Learn what the responsibilities are of a husband and wife, which can be found under the teaching and preaching of a good, Bible-believing church pastor.

Understanding and implementing your roles will definitely change your relationship within your marriage.

- Husbands – Love your wife.[22]
- Wives – Submit to your husbands.
- Children – Obey your parents.

By identifying your problem areas, committing to change, dedicating to effective communication, working to keep your love alive, forgiving and forgetting... you will be well on your way to a healthy relationship, one in which you can begin anew to start right, stay right and finish right.

Those bad crops will mature for harvest and eventually die off. God is merciful, loving, and gracious, and it never hurts to ask Him for crop failure! There's been so many times in my own life when I haven't reaped what I have sown. God has been merciful to me, a sinner... and since God made the *Laws of Sowing and Reaping*, He can change them at His will.

"The Lord is merciful and gracious, slow to anger, and plenteous in mercy. He will not always chide: neither will he keep his anger forever. He hath not dealt with us after our sins; nor rewarded us according to our iniquities. For as the heaven is high above the earth, so great is his mercy towards them that fear him. As far as the east is from the west, so far hath he removed our transgressions from us."

Psalms 103:8-11

Chapter 6

Society's View of Marriage

Fifty-one.

That's the percentage of marriages that end in divorce.[1] Out of 100 marriages, only 49 of them will last the lifelong marathon. Scary, huh? Even more troubling is the fact that 67% of second marriages and 74% of third marriages end in divorce!

It's no wonder there is a record-breaking number of unmarried couples living together, more than ever before in human history. In 2008, there were 5.5 million male-female couples living together in the United States of America. In 2009, that figure increased to 6.7 million and increased further still, to 7.5 million in 2010.

The United States of America has the highest cohabitation rate in the world. In contrast, the lowest percentage cohabitation rate is found in Israel; less than 3%.[2] *"Shacking up"* has steadily increased over the last 30 years, but the sudden rate of increase has surprised even the experts.

"The changing views of family are being driven largely by young adults 18 to 29 who are more likely than older generations to have an unmarried or divorced parent or have friends who do. Young adults also tend to have more liberal attitudes when it comes to spousal roles and living together before marriage. Economics factors, too, are playing a role."

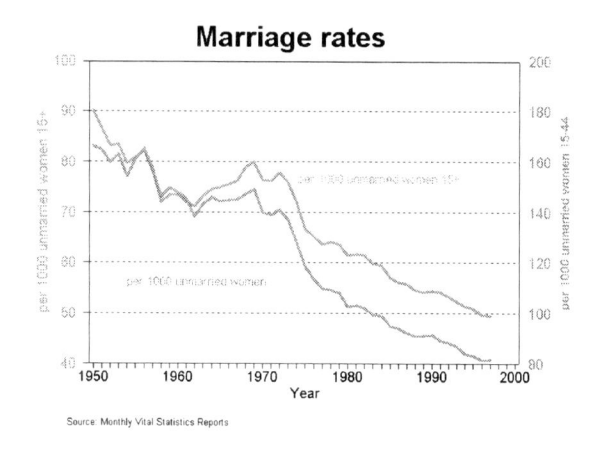

> While speaking to a single, young service member about marrying, he stated, "Why should I get married when it will only end in divorce? My parents got a divorce. My brother got a divorce.
>
> My sister's going through a divorce. My First Sergeant is divorced.
>
> It seems like everyone is getting a divorce nowadays. Me and my girlfriend are living together so that if it doesn't work out, we can go our separate ways and move on."
>
> His attitude about marriage is what I call the "renter's" approach to marriage. If you have no long-term commitment in your heart and mind, you'll have no lifetime investment in your marriage.

In September of 2010, released U.S. census data showed that marriages hit an all-time low. Only 52% of adults (18 and over) are tying the marital knot.[3] It's becoming acceptable to live together, so much so that society no sees anything morally wrong with it. Yet in America's not too distant past, property owners would deny unmarried couples to rent from them. In 2015, half of U.S. states explicitly prohibit discrimination based marital status, but in the other half, a property owner can still legally refuse to rent to an unmarried couple.

One article on this subject reads:

> *State laws prohibiting cohabitation typically use words like lewd and lascivious, public scandal, disgrace, "crime against public morals and decency." These laws were written generations ago, and no longer reflect citizen's values. Nonetheless, in these states a cohabiting different-sex couple can be charged with a crime, fined and imprisoned!*[4]

As you can tell from this article, the *"living in sin"* stigma has almost completely died out in the last 30 years and anyone that speaks out against it will labeled as using *hate speech*.[5]

Marrying and sticking it out is becoming rare, but those that are determined to work at their marriage will be blessed of the Lord. The Word of God uses powerful words like "steadfast" and "unmovable" to describe the characteristics of a person with their mind made up![6] They have rock solid determination that, "come hell or high water," they are committed to their marriage, they will fight for their marriage and they will not be moved from their firm foundation.

What is a Marriage?

Society's view of both marriage and family in the United States of America has changed dramatically within the last 100 years. If you would have asked the same question up unto the 1960's, any person in America could have given the definition of *marriage* and *family*. Yet when we, as a nation, move further away from Truth, the clear, unadulterated definition of marriage is questioned, challenged and changed until there is no clear definition at all.[7]

In 1828, Noah Webster defined marriage in the dictionary as:

1. The act of uniting **man and woman** for life; wedlock; the legal union of a man and woman for life.

2. Marriage was instituted by God himself for the purpose of preventing the promiscuous intercourse of the sexes, for promoting domestic felicity, and for securing the maintenance and education of children.

3. Marriage is honorable and the bed undefiled. Heb. 13.

4. In the Scriptural sense, the union between Christ and his church by the covenant of grace. Rev. 19.

Wow! I like old Noah Webster. So descriptive. So clear. So complete. So righteous. Yet that was in 1828. How could it possibly change in less than 200 years?

The following definition of marriage comes from the 2010 *Webster Dictionary* (no longer of Noah Webster)...

1. The state of being united to a person of the opposite sex as husband or wife in a consensual and contractual relationship recognized by law.

2. The state of being united to a person of the **same sex** in a relationship

Marriage is a Four-Letter Word

like that of traditional marriage <same-sex marriage>.

In less than 200 years, our dictionaries don't read the same. Someone has pulled a *fast one* on us. With God *out* of the picture, society has determined that the definition of marriage is:

- No longer restricted to a man and woman.
- No longer instituted by God.
- No longer honorable.
- No longer Scriptural.
- No longer a picture of Christ and His church.

It's a sad day in America when we can't figure out what marriage is! That's what happens when you have an absence of God – the very one who gave us the definition of marriage and the establishment of family structure in the very beginning with the creation of one man and one woman – Adam and Eve, not Adam and Steve.

The anatomy of the human body clearly presents the fact that a woman fits together with a man, just like a lock and a key or a plug and a socket. Two people of the same sex simply don't fit together... period! Men have an external sexual organ and women an internal. As a key is to a lock, so is man to woman. Any six-year-old can tell you the difference!

To think that anything else is *"natural"* means that you have denied the natural desires that God put in your heart for the opposite sex, and/or deliberately justified those that choose that type of lifestyle by substituting society's philosophies for God's design.[8] Even nature itself teaches that the female and male are designed for each other.

What is family? Since culture has blurred the definition of marriage, why wouldn't it do the same with the definition of a family? What constitutes a family anyhow? A 2010 national survey concluded that four out of five surveyed indicated that unmarried, opposite-sex couples with children constituted a family. Three out of five stated that a same-sex couple with children was a family.[9]

Chapter 6. Society's View of Marriage

What Happened?

Society's views and definitions of both marriage and family are fundamentally warped. The very fabric, framework and foundation of marriage has been diluted and distorted by mass media such as television programs and Hollywood movies, which are the main culprits that have done more damage to the structure of marriage and family in the last decade than in the entire history of humankind.

> **FACT: Oklahoma has the highest rate of people who have been married three times or more.**[10]

According to statistics, the United States of America, whose motto is *"In God We Trust,"* is the leading nation in divorce, and has the highest percentage of divorce rate in all of the world.[11] Wow! We are number one, and it's not any statistic to be proud of! Lost in the shuffle is the average American who is completely unaware of the *war against marriage* that is propagated, publicized, advertised and promoted on a daily basis.

Here are some statistical facts from the last one hundred years of American history:[12]

1900 - 2000

1. The number of marriages have increased 4.5% due to the population increase.

2. The adult population has also increased 4.5%, yet considerably less adults are marrying... to the tune of 30 million.

3. Although there are more marriages now due to a larger population, there are also more divorces! The divorce rate has increased 108% in 100 years.

US Population from 1900 to 2010

1900 - 76,212,168
1910 - 92,228,496
1920 - 106,021,537
1930 - 123,202,624
1940 - 132,164,569
1950 - 151,325,798
1960 - 179,323,175
1970 - 203,211,926
1980 - 226,545,805
1990 - 248,709,873
2000 - 281,421,906
2010 - 309,161,581

Marriage is a Four-Letter Word

Statistical data concludes...

- In 1900 there were 198,000 divorced adults.
- In 2000 there were 21,560,000 divorced adults!

Some of you are old enough to remember a time when divorce was not so common. In fact, it was shameful. In the '50s and '60s you could count on one hand the number of kids you knew whose parents were divorced. If it happened in your neighborhood, everyone knew about it.

It's not so nowadays. Today you can drive around your neighborhood and expect that, for every home with a married couple, there is a home right beside it with a divorced spouse. 29% of children are being raised by a divorced or never-married parent; a five-fold increase from 1960![13]

Think about all the people you know who have experienced divorce. You know who they are. They're friends, parents, family members, neighbors, and perhaps you. You could write your own book with a list of names and dates:

John	&	Becky	. Married 7 years. Divorced.
_____	&	_____	. Married ___ years. Divorced.
_____	&	_____	. Married ___ years. Divorced.
_____	&	_____	. Married ___ years. Divorced.

> **Facebook is driving the divorce rate up. ~ FOX News (June 2010)**[14]

It's disheartening to see how accepted, promoted and glamorized divorce is made out to be in the media. The entertainment tabloids make millions from their trash gossip about which Hollywood couples are divorcing, who's separating, who's getting the house, who's ending up with the Mercedes, who gets the children, who gets the dog, and definitely who gets all the money.

All around us, we are bombarded with divorce. Media such as *People Magazine*, *Entertainment Weekly* and *Star Magazine* boast about the *famous celebrity* divorces in their headlines:[15]

1. Rupert Murdoch's divorce from Anna Murdoch - *"The most expensive divorce in history"* at $1.7 billion
2. Tiger Woods' divorce from Elin Nordegren - $750 million

Chapter 6. Society's View of Marriage

3. Michael Jordan's divorce from Juanita Jordan - $150 million
4. Neil Diamond's divorce from Marcia Murphey - $150 million
5. Harrison Ford's divorce from Melissa Mathison - $118 million
6. Greg Norman's divorce from Laura Andrassy - $103 million
7. Steven Spielberg's divorce from Amy Irving - $100 million
8. Madonna's divorce from Guy Ritchie - $90 million
9. Kevin Costner's divorce from Cindy Silva - $80 million
10. Kenny Rogers' divorce from Marianne Rogers - $60 million
11. James Cameron's divorce from Linda Hamilton - $50 million
12. Paul McCartney's divorce from Heather Mills - $48.6 million
13. Michael Douglas' divorce from Diandra Douglas - $45 million
14. Ted Danson's divorce from Casey Coates - $30 million
15. Donald Trump's divorce from Ivana Trump - $25 million
16. Lionel Richie's divorce from Diane Richie - $20 million
17. Mick Jagger's divorce from Jerry Hall - $15 to $25 million.

The Seven-Year Itch

I taught a marriage seminar in the beautiful Olympic city of Lake Placid, New York and asked 78 couples, "How many of you think that the first years of marriage are the toughest?" Approximately 50 hands went up. "Of you that have your hands up," I inquired, "How many of you have been married more than five years?"

All but 6-10 hands went down.

"We have a lot of young couples that haven't yet experienced longevity in the marriage," I said. "What the rest of you more mature couples realize is that the young couples still have some rough times ahead."

Trends in counseling and divorce statistics conclude that the first year of marriage is not the most difficult. Sure, it may be challenging in learning and

Marriage is a Four-Letter Word

adjusting to each other, but the increasing trends indicate that years six, seven and eight are the most difficult. It's during these later years that husband and wife begin to recognize that the luster of marriage has worn off. Their love for each other has faded with time, and their spouse just doesn't create the excitement (*the butterflies*) that he/she once did.

The husband rarely surprises his wife with flowers, a spa certificate, or a sensual evening out on the town. He communicates more through grunts and burps than he does through talking. His idea of intimacy is one of self-gratification, with little regard for her satisfaction. He takes his wife for granted.

The wife wears the same nightgown/pajamas that she's had for the last two years. She no longer takes the time to be sexy, nor does she surprise her husband with unplanned intimacy. Why? It's too much work. All her energy has been zapped by the labor of cleaning up after him and taking care of the children. She also works and it's all just so complicated. Her love has also faded away.

This is a time in a marriage when couples experience what's known as the *"seven-year itch."* It's when a husband or wife recognizes the downward trend and they try to spice things up with their spouse. Some couples seek counseling. Some try to make changes themselves more attractive to solicit the interest of their spouse. They may join a gym, spend $5,000 on cosmetic surgery, change their hairstyle, and/or purchase a new wardrobe – all because they desperately want to get out of the marital rut.

It's at this point that many spouses are no longer attracted to the one they married seven years prior, but still want a change in their direction. They still want love, but just don't *feel* it from their spouse.

It's a very dangerous and susceptible time in a spouse's life. A time when they want change but are not getting any from their spouse. A time when the opposite sex, at this opportune moment, under just the right circumstances, can insert themselves into the mix and cause a mess. That person is usually:

1. A co-worker, or...
2. A close friend, or…
3. A past lover, and is usually...
4. Known to both the husband and wife.

Chapter 6. Society's View of Marriage

At this six, seven, or eight year mark, couples are deciding if they really want to *fight* for their marriage or take *flight* (separate and divorce).

It's about this time that couples have settled comfortably into their marriage. The luster and lust between the husband and wife are gone. They have children, careers, carriages, cottages and caretakers, but live unhappily because of circumstances. They have failed to keep the love alive. They have failed to identify problem areas and work through them to solve them. They entertain the thoughts of *"fight or flight."* Both are defensive tactic terms used to describe actions taken to protect (fight) or simply run away (flight).

"Do I fight for this marriage, or do I call it quits and walk away?"

> **"Marriage is something worth fighting for!"**[16] ~ *Evangelist Phil Schipper*

Some couples decide to fight for the marriage, and many others consider it not worth fighting for. Whatever the case, it's decision-making time. Those that divorce often claim that it was time to *get out* of the relationship before investing another eight to ten years into it. Others believe it's the best time to divorce, before the children get older.

Then there are those who believe that they still have a shot at another relationship if they divorce before they get much older. Some have suffered through the years of marriage and have held on so long hoping for change that never came that eventually, something had to give.

Those that push past these difficult years are in it for the long haul. Perhaps their relationship isn't great, but, as they think, *"It could always be worse."* Others are strapped down financially or obligatorily and can't see a way out at the time. Some hang in there hoping that their spouse will change. Yet nearly all of them hang on longest for the sake of…you guessed it…the children.

Values

There is an ever-increasing divorce rate of couples married for 15, 20 and 25 years. The last three I encountered:

Marriage is a Four-Letter Word

- One husband was being divorced by his wife of 30 years.
- One husband was divorced at 25 years.
- One woman was abandoned by her husband after 22 years of marriage.

So why the trend in marriages divorcing after 15 years, and especially the 20- to 25-year mark? The reason is quite simpler than you may believe. It comes down to values instilled, values gained, and values influenced.

1. Values instilled - as a child.

2. Values gained – as a teen and young adult.

3. Values influenced - by society as a whole.

If you had negative values concerning marriage instilled or gained while growing up, you're more likely to divorce. Those negative values could be a broken home, absence of a parent figure, rejection, etc. If you don't know what a happy, successful marriage looks like, how are you expected to keep one together yourself?

Then, as an adult, if your good values are negatively influenced by society's view of marriage, you're more susceptible to divorce. Any decent, moral, Biblical values instilled growing up can be deteriorated by a society that no longer values marriage. Your view of *right* may be diminished and you may find yourself going through a divorce that you thought you'd never go through.

> **For all the premarital counseling and wedding ceremonies I've been a part of, not one couple ever dreamt of divorcing!**

At the time of this publication, the majority of couples married for 15-25 years are in the age brackets of 40-55. They were born between the years of 1955 and 1970, in an era that was beginning to experience a rapid increase in divorce rates, yet still had decent values of love, marriage and long-term commitment brought about by an earlier and more stable World War II generation.

Prior to WWII women rarely worked outside the home but the war era demanded the increased production of "*beans and bullets*" (war supplies) which drove many a mother and wife to the factories. The end of the war did not end the movement of women in the workplace. Marriages began to

Chapter 6. Society's View of Marriage

experience the power of two incomes, as opposed to one and added stressors began to take a toll on relationships.

It was these post WWII marriages that produced a baby boom generation who were teens and young adults of the 1960s, with the war era of Vietnam. This was an entirely new generation of free love, free will and freethinking, accommodated by the widespread usage of hallucinogen drugs. This generation was the first to experience the full wake of the breakdown in the family structure, as many a mother and father never recovered to *normalcy* of the family structure after WWII.

Throughout the 1960s, and increasingly into the 1970s, the downward decline of marriage tore at the family seams. Although marriage was tested and tried in the '60s and especially the '70s, the divorce figures were not at all what they are today, some four decades later, and eight decades since WWII. Remember, even though divorce was becoming more common in the '60s and '70s, very few families in the neighborhood were divorced.

At the turn of the 20th century, children are increasingly exposed to so much divorce that it seems more common than uncommon. Marriage, to them, is uncommon. In fact, 50% of children today are void of what a *normal*, functional family looks like, because their lives have been anything but normal. We have a generation that is raised in split homes without any good example of what a normalcy is.

Our nation's children are exposed to so much divorce that it's almost more common to dissolve marriage or *split apart* than to stay together. Yet any adult age 50 or over can clearly see what changes have taken place over the years. If you are 50 or older, you remember. You were raised on at a time when marriage was still considered somewhat sacred and respectable by a national majority that desired to *stick it out* and *make it work*. Why? Because a vow meant something!

If your marriage makes it past the *"seven-year itch"* and it's still not what it should be...hold on because there's more surprises ahead. Many who continue to stay together and *stick it out* or *make it work* for 15 - 25 years are not keeping the love alive. The kids grow up and move out, some to college,

Marriage is a Four-Letter Word

some to the military the military, some to the basement, and some are still *finding themselves.* For the first time in two decades, a husband and wife are left to themselves and they realize that they have absolutely nothing in common anymore. The marital glue that held them together has dissolved. They have their own separate careers, hobbies and interests. The bills are paid. The cars are paid off. The stress is low, but they no longer share common bonds or connections. They lack intimacy. The love has died. Perhaps the only thing that they have in common is the household dog.

It's at this time that one, the other, or both together realize that they don't want to be married to the person across from them. Regardless (and without much remorse), they divorce. Teens still living at home are devastated, hurt, angry and bitter. Those that have moved on are also affected by the news. The rest of us hear of these 20-year marriages blowing apart and say, *"I can't believe it!"*

Whatever society claims, the world as a whole or the media determines about marriage and the family, decide that your perception will not be influenced by their view. Your view must be that of God, which hasn't changed since the beginning of the creation. People change. Human definitions change. Marriages change. Couples within the marriage change.

> *"And the world passeth away, and the lust thereof: but he that doeth the will of God abideth for ever."* I John 2:17

So build your life on the only one that will be a foundation of consistency in your marriage – the Lord Jesus Christ.

> *"For I am the LORD, I change not…"* Malachi 3:6

> *"Jesus Christ the same yesterday, and today, and forever."*
> Hebrews 13:8

Chapter 7

The Missing Family Table

Y ou've heard the term, *"The family that prays together stays together."* What, exactly, does it mean to you? What is it about the family that actually brings them together in unity?

According to Holy Scripture, prayer brings unity with God and with each other.[1] When there is unity, communication will flow effectively, order can be maintained, tasks can be accomplished, and love can thrive. Thus, a family that prayers together is nearly inseparable – but in order for a family to pray together, they must come together... and that may be a challenge!

The purpose of this chapter is to describe how the average family's structure has eroded, and to equip you with suggestive tools to bring your family together with stronger bonds.

Just for a moment, think about your dinner table. Visualize it. Is it wood or metal? Four chairs or eight? Is it cluttered or clean? Can you eat a meal at it right now?

The dining room table is something that most families are missing nowadays. Missing – as in no longer using! There used to be a time when American families routinely ate supper together several times a week, but for the average family those times are now few and far between.

Now, think back to the old television programs such as *Leave It to Beaver, Little House on the Prairie, The Lucille Ball Show* and *The Andy Griffith Show*. Remember how the families ate dinner together? It was a common occurrence. Yet by 2015, the average family didn't come together more than

Marriage is a Four-Letter Word

once a week. Statistically speaking, if you didn't come together for a family meal while growing up as a child, chances are that you won't bring your family together as an adult.

> **59% of adults say that their family today has fewer family dinners than when they were growing up[2]**

Some of you (myself included) remember playing outside as a young person. When it was time for supper, you could hear Mom's voice calling or a dinner bell ringing from a mile away. It signaled us that Dad had come home and dinner was almost ready. All the kids in the neighborhood expected supper between 5 - 6 p.m.! It was standard procedure.

Remember all the chores to be done in preparation for supper, such as setting the table and pouring the drinks? Mom would never fail to remind us, *"Don't forget to wash your hands!"* I remember being taught the correct order of the knife, fork and spoon, and on which side of the plate to place the drinking glass. After the meal, there were more chores to be done, such as clearing the table, washing dishes and taking out the trash.

It was this kind of mealtime interaction that brought families close together. But when family mealtime is replaced by Dish TV, iPods, iPhones, laptops, tablets, Game Boys, magazines any family structure built will slowly disintegrate over time.

Supper (or dinner depending whether you're from the north or the south) should be an important time for every family, and is specifically important for the influence and structure of the children. So if you want to united your home, build family structure and have a long-lasting family....bring back the dinner table and eat together routinely.

Here's why the average family rarely comes together more than once a week:

1. Dad works late, so Mom's never certain when to cook and have dinner prepared.
2. Mom works also, and even if she's home in time to cook supper, that time is filled with...
    - Picking up little Johnny from Child Care...

Chapter 7. The Missing Family Table

- Taking Suzie to soccer practice, and...
- Picking up the eldest from football practice.

3. Since Mom and Dad don't communicate well enough to plan evening meals, it seems to be easier for everyone to *get their own food*, while Mom takes care of household chores. Hence the phrase, *"every man for himself."*

4. Additionally, who says that Mom has to be the one to cook anyhow? She's worked just as hard as her husband all day long, so why can't he cook? The responsibilities of the family members are not equally shared.

5. Meanwhile, Dad usually comes home from work tired, plops on the couch, kicks off his boots and turns to ESPN for the rest of the evening. If that's not enough, he turns to the computer. He's no more interested in dinner with the family than he is in playing soccer with Suzie in the backyard. When he's ready to eat supper, it's easier to get his own food than fight with his wife about it.

6. Suzie doesn't bother Dad with games because there's never been a family "bond" between them. She's volunteer prisoner of her room where her life consists of Facebook, Myspace, her music and her cell phone.

7. Big John has no reason or incentive to come home so he hangs out with his friends watching movies, eating with them. When he does come home, he also hangs out in his room strumming his guitar or spending endless hours playing on his games.

8. Little Johnny wants all the attention and follows Mom around everywhere, so she can't get a break. She tells him to go play with Dad but that's short-lived because Dad only plays during the commercials. Little Johnny loves his older siblings but they chase

him out of their rooms because he's a nuisance and invades their privacy. It seems that his greatest influences are cartoons and his best friend is the family dog.

9. Before this dysfunctional family realizes it, the evening is spent almost entirely without family interaction of any kind. No meals, games, prayers, or real interaction has been spent together. The next day the cycle continues all over again.

10. Big John and Suzie will soon move on to a job, the military or college. Eventually they will marry and begin their own families. With no example of what the family structure is supposed to look like, they are doomed to falling into the same rut as their mother and father, and a rut is nothing more than a grave with both ends kicked out. Their only hope is to find out what the correct family structure and interaction looks like, embrace and incorporate it into their marriage, and break the mold from whence they came.

The Family Table

Your family table is a reflection of your family relationship. Envision your family table once again. If you can see it from where you are sitting, look at it. How cluttered is it? Can you find it underneath the clutter? Is it a magnet for bills, newspapers, computers and unnecessary junk? Or is it a magnet for the family to come together and interact?

Does your family table welcome, or repel visitors? Does it bring your family closer, or push them away? A cluttered table is a direct reflection of a disorganized and cluttered life. Perhaps you have too much going on that you can't slow down, to enjoy the simple pleasures of family time.

If you want to bring health to a family, take the kitchen garbage container and put it next to your family table. Now push all of your clutter into the can. Clear your table for children, wife and husband. Clear your table for relatives, neighbors and friends. Clear your table and thereby create some space for the ones you love the most.[3]

If you have a family table that's not cluttered... how often is it used? Perhaps

Chapter 7. The Missing Family Table

it's only eye candy for friends and associates that come to your home. It's delicately and neatly arranged with fine china, crystal glasses and cloth napkins. It looks great, but it's rarely used. It's more of a façade than it is a family table.

> **The marital rut is nothing more than a grave with both ends kicked out.**

Maybe you have a measure of wealth, a good position in your line of work and generally good health. You have morals, and values, and education, and motivation. If your family table has become one of impression rather than interaction... it's worthless! Get back to using it for its intended function.

Bring back family time in your marriage by bringing back the family table. Work together with your spouse to schedule at least four or more evening meals each week as a family. It will change your family and it will burn the image in the minds of your children, and help keep the love alive with your spouse.

The Family Table...

- Stimulates interaction
- Increases communication
- Creates good practice
- Trains the children about what a family together looks like
- Affords the children a time of interaction and learning
- Establishes rules and boundaries
- Allows for future plans to be made
- Communicates schedules to be synced
- Unites the family together in prayer
- Demonstrates and reinforces family values
- Creates life-lasting strong bonds of unity

The next section contains suggestions to increase family relations at the dinner table.

Table Time

I had a friend tell me that they spend no less than one hour together at the family table.[4] "Wow!" I thought, "I need to work on that." They served dinner in three main courses, and did not move on to the next course until the family was finished.

Another spouse told me that their family ate together at least four times a week, but shamefully admitted that the purpose was not for interaction and relationship strengthening, but rather to quickly finish and move on to other projects.

Consider the purpose of coming together as a family as being far more substantial than just to feed the body. The time you spend together is character forming for the entire family. It's the time to learn and grow from each other by interacting. It's the time to laugh and enjoy one another's company. It's a time to feed the family spiritually and emotionally.

It's no wonder that the family table has dissolved! Our reasons for coming together have changed. We are more interested in eating than socializing.

Spend more time at the dinner table today and you'll spend less time wondering why you don't have anything in common with your kids tomorrow.

Love & Lead

Dad, husbands, men... as the leader of your home, it's your responsibility to lead the family in love. You lead while your wife guides. Although your wife would be like the rudder that steers a great ship, you are at the helm. That doesn't mean that anyone is less important, it simply means that the dinner table is the greatest moment for the children to see the family structure as it should be – as God intended it to be.

Chapter 7. The Missing Family Table

> **Strong families are built on strong men**

Every business, every military unit, every corporation has a leader. Someone must lead and others must follow. The followers aren't any less important, because without the followers, there would be no one to lead.

The Lord established the home in the same fashion, with the husband as the leader – so men, if you don't lead your family, someone else in the family will.[5] Wives, if you don't like this established hierarchy, you are in opposition to God's plan. If your husband is a knucklehead, there are ways that God will deal with him, and there are methods for dealing with him.[6] Lastly, children are to be in obedience to their parents which means that mother and father need to be on the same communication wavelength when it comes to rules and discipline.[7]

> *"Husbands, love your wives…"*
>
> *"Wives, submit yourselves to your own husbands…"*
>
> *"Children, obey your parents…"*
>
> Ephesians 5:21, 25; 6:1

> **Family Table Tip: Husbands take the lead on gathering your family together for dinner. This positive role demonstrates loving leadership to the children.**

Appreciate

A method to show appreciation for members of the family is to have a special dinner plate that's different from all the rest. The plate may be formed differently or a different color, but whatever the case, make the plate known as *"The Special Plate."* At each family meal, pass the plate to the next family

Cool Monkey

member. The one who receives the special plate now becomes the "*special person*" for the meal. Each family member shows their appreciation to the special person by telling them what they love so much about them.

Example:

> Dad: "Izak, you get the special plate tonight and each says one reason why we love you. Who wants to go first?
>
> Mom: "Izak, I love you because you were good at school today."
>
> Jordan: "I love you, Izak, because you stayed out of my room!"
>
> Levi: "I luv you 'cause… um… um… 'cause you let me play with your Hot Wheels toys."
>
> Dad: "Izak, I love you because you're a smart, handsome, awesome young man."

Lastly, the "*special*" person prays. You would be remarkably surprised at how special the prayers are once your child feels appreciated! This process boosts their confidence in themselves and increases their love for the family. It burns into their memory what the family structure looks like, and the values that accompany it.

Sing

Especially true in Christian homes, singing Christian songs and hymns brings the family closer together. The first time that I was exposed to singing at the dinner table in my dear friend's home in Davao, Philippines in 2005. I participated with great humility and admiration as Dr. Claro Loquias Sr., the Hudson Taylor of Mindanao, led his family at dinner time.[8]

As I sat at their family table with his wife Alice, surrounded by their sons, daughters, and a slew of grandchildren, I was deeply impressed that absolutely nothing, other than God Himself, was more important than family. We joined hands and they began to sing simple, yet heartfelt songs

> **God's into math. He always seeks to multiply, add and unite. Satan divides and subtracts.**

Chapter 7. The Missing Family Table

of thanks to the Lord. I felt out of place. I had never experienced this before – no, not even with my own family.

I embraced their family values and brought this intimacy back to my family in the United States. We now sing before our meals and it has made a noticeable, measurable difference. Quite often, the family is excited to pick the song that all the family will sing together, especially the younger children. The two favorite songs at our dinner table are "Jesus Loves Me" and "I'll Fly Away." If you are a guest, family or friend at our dinner table… prepare to sing a song and experience this with us.

Pray

Prayer is a spiritual proponent that brings a family together.

- Having problems with your marriage? Are you praying together?
- Having problems with your teen? Are you praying together?

You see, it's tough to pray together and remain distant, closed or opposed to one another. God always seeks to multiply, add and unite...but Satan divides and subtracts.

The dinner table is a great place for your child to hear mom and dad pray, and it's a good opportunity to teach them how to pray, just like Jesus did His disciples.[9] Dinner time is when we thank the Lord for each member of the family and immediate family members with issues of concern (health, etc.). It teaches respect for grandparents and putting the needs of others before your own.

Prayers for meals don't need to be long and lengthy. It's not a Wednesday night prayer meeting at church. This is not the time to attempt to impress your family or guest, nor is it the time to make up for your lack of prayer throughout your day.

It is good, however, to ask, *"Who has a special prayer requests?"* This allows your children to think about and remember the needs of others. Your children will come up with some good requests! *"Pray for Grandma's hip to get better." "Pray for uncle Micah in Afghanistan." "Pray for me to do well on my test at school tomorrow."* You may need to solicit prayer requests to get them thinking, such as, *"Before we eat, we pray. Before we pray, we need two prayer requests. Who has one?"* Usually though, after incorporating this practice into your family table time, everyone will begin to know what's expected when they sit down….even the teens.

Remember why you are praying:

1. To thank God for the provision of food.
2. To ask for His blessing on the food (there's a curse on it[10]).
3. To pray for others.
4. To teach your children, by example, what a real Christian family looks like so when they grow up and move out, they'll follow your example.

Bring prayer from the heart as you use it to teach your children what a relationship (not religion) with God is all about.

Communicate

The main purpose of coming together around the family table is to talk and interact. Expect it from your children. Ask them about their day at school. Talk to your spouse about their day at work and/or home. Plan future activities. Give kind comments and praise to your family. Ask open-ended questions that require more than a yes or no answer.

Instead of asking, "*Did you have a good day at school?*" try, "*Tell me about your day at school*," or "*What was the best part of your day?*"

This special table time together is not the time to argue, fuss or fight. This is the time of effective, joyful, meaningful talk – vertically, horizontally, around and across the table. This is one of the very best moments for your children (of all ages) to see how you interact with your spouse. They are burning a mental picture on their brain of how a man treats a woman and a woman treats a man; of how a husband treats a wife and a wife treats a husband. What they bring away from the family table is what will influence them throughout their lifetime.

Rational

What type of food did you despise growing up? Did you like asparagus? How about liver or onions? Mushrooms? Yuck! I despise liver, mushrooms, onions, and lima beans. No special method of cooking them can make me like them. It's not going to happen. If I had my way, I'd never buy them, cook them or eat them for the rest of my life. It wouldn't bother me one bit. If I was forced to eat them as a Prisoner of War, or if I was at someone's home and they served them, I would politely take my share and get it over.

> **"If mom cooks it, we all try it. Everyone gets at least one spoonful of everything, because anyone can put down one spoonful."**
> ~Evangelist Philip Schipper[11]

You (like me) may have children that simply don't like certain types of food. Expect that there are some things they can't overcome, but teach them to *"wash down what you don't like."*

Here's why…

The last situation you'd want to be placed in is to be the dinner guest in someone's home, and your children become an embarrassment when they blurt out, "Ewwww. I don't like that" and refuse to eat it. Your children should be trained to take a minimum of one spoonful of everything cooked – like it or not, period. Everyone can choke down a spoonful.

There is a difference between being a picky (fussy, meticulous) eater and not liking something. A picky eater will like hot dogs one day but not the next. A picky eater will eat macaroni today, and complain about it tomorrow. Cultivating picky-eating-children is what you want to avoid.

Know the difference between your child being a picky eater and simply not liking something. There will be times when the child will need to sit at the table until they eat it. It may come down to the child's will against yours. If your child is still sitting there 15 minutes after the table is cleared… not eating, then it's time to figure out if they are being a picky eater or they just don't like it.

Be consistent. If you require everyone to take a spoonful, then you take a spoonful. If you make your child "sit there until they eat it," do just that. Don't baby them. Don't give an alternative after you made your decision. Don't keep warming the food up in the microwave just because it's cold. They let it get cold. Remember that you're molding and building your children with character traits that will last throughout life.

Teamwork

Work together to make it a joyous occasion. Instead of demanding another family member to get an item out of the refrigerator, give of yourself to do it. Don't expect Mom to do everything. She's not a slave or the family chef. She's the queen and the mother of the family.

If there's an accident, such as a spill, don't overreact, as I have been guilty of in the past! Messes happen all the time with kids. Remember, your children are taking mental notes of the family interaction and what you show them is what they think it's supposed to look like. Help with the messes and join in the cleanup.

Manners

Establish some *table manners* that everyone knows and abides by such as:
- Don't chew with your mouth open.

Chapter 7. The Missing Family Table

- Don't talk with your mouth full.
- Don't reach over someone's plate.
- Don't wipe your mouth on your sleeve.
- Don't get into a burping contest with your siblings.
- Don't eat with your hands.
- Don't throw food.
- Cover your mouth when you cough or sneeze.
- Finish what food you have before asking for more.
- Ask politely for something to be passed.
- Don't interrupt someone while they are talking.
- Ask to be excused when finished or needing to use the restroom.
- Put your plate in the sink.
- Clean up your area.

Have fun interacting at the table but maintain some decency. Allow it to be a relaxed atmosphere that's conducive to growth, learning and communication.

Responsibly

We all have things to do, places to be and projects to accomplish, but maintain control of keeping the family together until everyone is finished at the table. Require your children to ask to be excused. It's the proper and respectful method of character building.

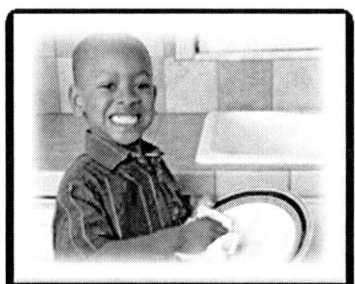

Your children of all ages should have some chores and responsibilities when they have finished eating. When the meal is complete, have your children take their plate to the kitchen, scrape it off in the trash and rinse it off in the sink. Place it in the dishwasher or in the appropriate sink.

Marriage is a Four-Letter Word

Every child should be able to complete this task by the age of three.

You can train toddlers to take their plate to the kitchen (with help), with a basic understanding of what goes in the garbage can and what goes in the sink. Have a stool handy so they can reach the sink. Teach them responsibility and make this a mealtime habit.

Designate children for tasks, such as putting items back in the refrigerator, pushing in the chairs, sweeping the floor or taking out the garbage. Again, Mom is not the maid. Help out.

Give directions and responsibility based on the ages. If everyone pitches in with putting things away, the chore will be less demanding on any one person. It's called synergism.

Teens should be used to washing dishes or running a dishwasher. No feedback is required. Everyone should know how to put dishes, glasses and utensils away. Work together in unity to make dinnertime a great family event, enjoyable and prosperous for all.

Commit

Before deploying to Afghanistan in 2010, I pastored a Christian congregation at the main post chapel of Fort Drum, New York. As our body of believers grew in size, it became obvious that the growth that we experienced was due to entire families attending. Not just women and children, but men, women and children. My burden was for families, and my focus was on men being changed by the Word of God. When men's heart were moved for God, they began to lead their families in love.

Here is my top 10 list to get cold families warm, get the warm families hot, and keep the hot families hot.

1. Pray together more frequently, and not just at mealtimes.
2. Eat together as a family four times or more a week.
3. Sing a hymn together before you eat.
4. Hold family devotions at least once a week.
5. Shut off electronic devices one night a week (TV, Computer, etc.).

Chapter 7. The Missing Family Table

6. Show random acts of kindness to each of your family members weekly.
7. Memorize the 66 books of the Bible and Scripture together.
8. Attend church services together and discuss the topics throughout the week.
9. Spend personal time alone with each family member.
10. Play table games as a family.

....

Let's summarize what you've digested up to this point:

Chapter 1 - *Marriage is a Four-Letter Word* spoke of the essence of marriage, the four-letter word: work.

Chapter 2 - *Identifying Problems* dealt with identifying problems within a marriage.

Chapter 3 - *Eliminating Problems* identified words, phrases and attitudes that kill a marriage....and the methods to eliminate them.

Chapter 4 – *Marriage Killers* explained the laws of sowing and reaping in relation to starting the marriage off on the wrong foot.

Chapter 5 - *Start Right, Stay Right, Finish Right* explained how to begin the relationship correctly in order to finish the marathon of marriage.

Chapter 6 - *Society's View of Marriage* explained society's interpretation and definition of marriage; how and why it has changed over the years.

Chapter 7 - *The Missing Family Table* included a plea to bring back family interaction into your marriage and articulating how the family table has faded with time.

Marriage is a Four-Letter Word

Chapter 8

Improving the Marital Foxhole[1]

God designed the husband and wife with unique qualities, needs and roles within the marriage. Understanding how God designed us will help better understand the needs that husbands and wives must provide for.

Let's take some fundamentals of the battlefield and relate them to the focus that a marriage should have to win the conflict between being a contender for marital longevity and success, or a pretender.[2]

"*War is hell*" but marriage should never be *hell*.[3] The absence of peace is conflict and the purpose of war is to end conflict and bring peace.[4] Therefore, any conflicts within the marriage should be identified and eliminated, stemming from a desire for resolution and peace.

If you ever come to a point in your marriage where it seems like a *living hell*, then your love has long died. Your problems were never identified and eliminated. Someone is not putting the other first and the love has drifted.

....

In a real war, when U.S. soldiers advance upon, close in and seize ground from the enemy, a few fundamental actions remain ongoing throughout the battle:

1. Security.
2. Improvements to the fighting positions.

Applying this to marriage, all marriages require both security and consistent improvements to make them healthy and life lasting. It's something I call "*Improving the Marital Foxhole*."

Foxholes evolve from fighting positions. When soldiers move into close proximity of the enemy and seek to hold ground, they form a defensive perimeter by clearing a shallow, hasty fighting position that's no longer than two lengths of their weapon, one length wide, and no more than 12" deep

Marriage is a Four-Letter Word

(butt-stock). These fighting positions are temporary emplacements to protect, defend and hold ground that would otherwise be taken by the enemy. Over the course of hours, soldiers continue to improve these fighting positions with camouflage and sector sketches.

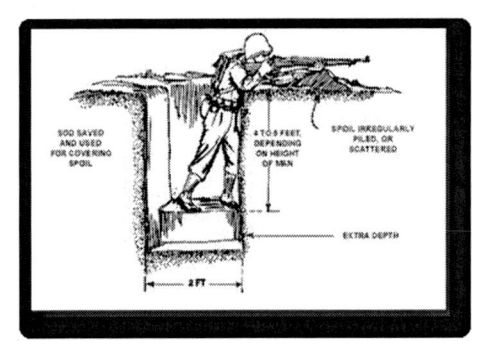

When the order is given to "stay put," "hold in place," or "dig in," these temporary fighting positions are dug into foxholes that are armpit deep. Some are fortified with overhead protection such as logs or sandbags, and many are connected together to form a trench. Improvements will continue over months and positions may be occupied for years, such as in the Vietnam War.

Grenade slumps will be dug, braces between the walls will be installed, ladders will be constructed, range sketches will be drawn, and ammunition points will be identified. Everything is carried out decently and in order, so that soldiers can effectively fight against the enemy and win... not just the battle, but also the war.

In the same sense, marriage is something worth fighting for![5] Take note: Marriage is NOT fighting against one another but against all the forces that seek to tear it apart at the very framework that brought it together. It's not something to be given up, laid down, or exchanged. Fight for it! I say again, fight for your marriage.

Understanding Roles

In order to provide security and make improvements to your marriage, you must first understand how the family is organized by God. The established order of the marriage is:

1. The Lord

Chapter 8. Improving the Marital Foxhole

2. The husband
3. The wife
4. The children.

This is the template that God prescribed and blesses. Establishing you home in this manner brings peace and protection.

> *"Wives, submit yourselves unto your own husbands, as unto the Lord. For the husband is the head of the wife, even as Christ is the head of the church: and he is the saviour of the body."* Ephesians 5:22-23

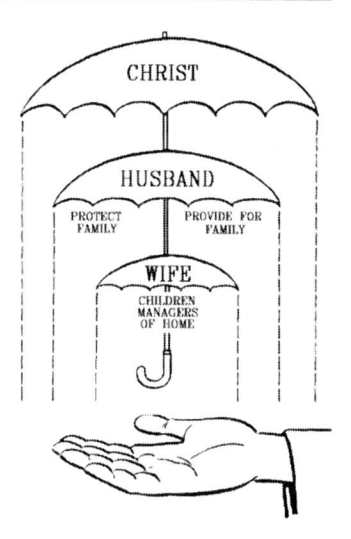

When the order is changed, you'll have disaster. It's like baking a cake but mixing up the order. If you throw the ingredients into a pan and bake it, only to pull it out of the oven and try to mix it, you'll end up with a kitchen disaster.

If the husband and wife both attempt to be the *"head"* of the marital body at the same time, you end up with a double-headed monster that will tear itself apart. Only one person can be the head, and the Lord gave the leadership position to the man from the very beginning when He presented Eve to Adam...

> *"And the LORD God said, It is not good that the man should be alone; I will make him an help meet for him."* Genesis 2:18

Woman was created to be the most suitable helper and enabler of the man. Perhaps you've heard the saying, *"Behind every good man is a great woman"* – and so it is true. Women – you are no less important because of your position as number two in the relationship! You are number one to your husband, and, in fact, you are so very important because of your position!

Behind every good man is a GREAT woman

Every organization, church, firm, business and club has a hierarchy. Every military squad, platoon, company, battalion, brigade, division and Corp has a leader. Someone's in charge. Someone is the commander or CEO. That doesn't mean that the second in command (executive officer or subordinates) is any less important! They are so very important as part of the team. A marital team that is in obedience to the basic God-designed, God-given structure of marriage is a marital team that is successful, solid and life lasting.

When men lead in love and women respect their husband's position by submitting and assisting, then the marriage will be embellished with peace, happiness, joy and love. Primary problems arise when husbands fail to lead in love. Someone has to take the helm, so who does it? The wives. It's not as God designed, but can you blame the wives for stepping up and filling in the gap?

Ladies, if your husband is a good-for-nothing loser - help him become a winner! You married him. You chose him. You picked him. You committed to him. You both said, "I do" so help him. Pray for him. Win him and don't be quick to give up. You have a promise from God to win him over.[6]

> A wise husband values his wife's input.

Husbands - if you are not stepping up to the plate and being the man you need to be, get with it! If you're the King, she's the Queen so treat her like a queen! Men often want to be the *king of the castle* yet forget that they are married to the queen. If you rule like a dictator, Drill Sergeant, First Sergeant or a shop supervisor, then expect to have some fallout with your spouse and kids. If that's the case, it's no wonder she has difficulty submitting to your authority! Where's the love? Where's the romance? Where's the shared leadership & responsibilities? Instead of cohesion and unity, you get mutiny.

The Scriptures speak clearly:

> *"Husbands, love your wives, even as Christ also loved the church, and gave himself for it."* Ephesians 5:25

When you love, you give! When you love, it shows! When you love,

Chapter 8. Improving the Marital Foxhole

your marriage grows!

Paul emphasizes the marriage relationship in the book of Ephesians, clearly defining our Lord Jesus Christ as the ultimate example of the one who freely and physically gave himself for believers – the true church. He's the only *head* of the church and the only Saviour of the body of believers.

> *"Jesus saith unto him, I am the way, the truth, and the life: no man cometh unto the Father, but by me."* John 14:6

> *"Neither is there salvation in any other: for there is none other name under heaven given among men, whereby we must be saved."* Acts 4:12

Therefore, the man is the head of the marriage, just as Christ is the head of the church and the husband's treatment of the wife should be in carefulness, sweetness with concern, cooperation and charity as unto Christ.

1. Christ gave his life for the church – the husband should be willing to give his life for his wife.
2. Christ did not disrespect the church – the husband should not disrespect his wife.
3. Christ never abused the church – the husband should never abuse his wife.
4. Christ never forsook the church – the husband should never leave or forsake his wife.
5. Christ defends the church – the husband should stick up for and defend his wife.
6. Christ forgives the church – the husband should have a forgiving heart for his wife.
7. Christ makes intercession for the church – the husband should come boldly before God for his wife.
8. Christ sets the greatest example for the church – the husband should set the greatest example for his wife.
9. Christ cares more about the church than himself – the husband should care more about his wife than himself.

> *"So ought men to love their wives as their own bodies. He that loveth his wife loveth himself. For no man ever yet hated*

Marriage is a Four-Letter Word

> *his own flesh; but nourisheth and cherisheth it, even as the Lord the church."* Ephesians 5:28-29

Wives – your relationship to your husband is vital to the marriage. You steer the home like a rudder on a ship with your husband at the helm. He turns the helm but you steer the family. You steer away from danger under his care.

Sin's curse established your husband as your ruler and leader... and it also established your love for him to lead.

> *"... and thy desire shall be to thy husband, and he shall rule over thee."*
> Genesis 3:16

When you submit to your husband, you are fulfilling his need for respect and you are honoring the Lord. When important decisions are complete, your husband's decision for the direction of the home should be the final say-so. Respect it. Abide by it. Honor it. Don't badger him until he changes his decision or give him the silent treatment. Don't withhold sex and never use it as a tool to get want you want from him. Work these things out in your marriage through effectively communicating, but realize that when the arguments have ended, it's the husband's decision that should be respected and honored.

I've been asked, "What if my husband doesn't lead like he's supposed to?" and "What if my husband doesn't make good decisions?" I tell you that you must remain consistent in your submission and respect to him because your husband will have to give an account to the Lord of how he led the home. Ladies, you don't have that load of responsibility. You are under the umbrella of God's protection if you continue to follow His design. You'll give account of how you submitted to and followed your husband's leadership. If he makes a bad decision and you submit to it, allow God to deal with your husband. Pray for him.

One of the methods by which God deals with us individually is through those "I told you so" moments, also known as "live and learn" moments.

Chapter 8. Improving the Marital Foxhole

Brian's "I told you so" story...

Early in our marriage my wife, Tracy, developed a compelling idea to sell Mary Kay cosmetics. She conducted her research and pitched her plan to me, describing all the details. My mind wandered off thinking about Mary Kay stickers on our vehicle, cosmetic parties during my football games, maybe a pink Cadillac in the driveway. I was abruptly snatched from my temporary delusion when she delivered her closing argument and I heard her say something about a $500 purchase of a starter kit. "Five hundred dollars!" I exclaimed, "No way!" Besides, Tracy was not the "seller" type. She couldn't sell a bucket of water to a man on fire. It's just not within her personality.

Okay, so I had my reasons, and perhaps I wasn't giving her the benefit of the doubt, but I was totally against it. Tracy was discouraged and I could tell. I never was one to crush her dreams and so I gave in within a few days. $500 later, we had a bedroom full of makeup, a few parties booked, but (thank God) no pink Mary Kay stickers on my truck! It seemed like sales would do fine if the pace continued, but just as quickly as most great ideas begin, so they end.

Within three months, the parties faded away and within six months they ceased to exist. Like the Atkins diet, Snuggy and the George Foreman Grill, this idea faded away like a bad memory. For the next 10 years (I kid you not), we had Rubbermaid storage boxes full of Mary Kay makeup invading our cramped spaces and following us with each household move. Today, it's a humorous subject that we can laugh about, but for many years, the words "I told you so" only started a fight.

> *"Likewise, ye husbands, dwell with them according to knowledge, giving honour unto the wife, as unto the weaker vessel..."* 1 Peter 3:7

It wasn't until years later that I realized I could have been more understanding and supportive to her ideas. Had I taken a greater interest in her interest, giving honor unto her and being more supportive, perhaps she would've been successful. I did nothing to promote, encourage or help her

Marriage is a Four-Letter Word

success, and it took years for me to realize how selfish I was not to take an active interest into something she really wanted to do.

Tracy's *"I told you so"* story ...

Men love big toys – and big toys have big price tags. Several years ago I was visited by the good-idea-fairy with a bright idea to purchase a snow thrower, but not just any snow thrower. I wanted a big one with a big engine, big tires and big controls. I shopped around and found the model I wanted at Lowes, and I went home excited to pitch my wife the plan to purchase it. I figured that I could make the purchase on the Lowes credit card, using the 12-month 0% interest plan, and pay it off in a couple of months with the money that I would make plowing driveways in the neighborhood – and perhaps even picking up a contract with a local business! Plus it would be a great opportunity to teach my son how to earn a living through hard work and persistency.

So, I pitched my plan and Tracy thought it was ridiculous. "You're going to go buy that snow thrower and it probably won't even snow this year!" she said, "We'll be stuck with a $1,000 bill that we don't need."

"Nonsense," I objected, "it will probably be a good year for snow, plus we only need a few jobs and we'll have the money in no time! It will pay itself off." With my overbearing positivism, I was certain that the plan would work!

She said, "Why can't you get a smaller one? Our driveway isn't that big anyhow, and we don't need to spend all that money on a snow blower!"

"It's only a few hundred dollars more than the smaller blower," I bargained, "Besides, we'll have it forever and we can use it if we ever move to a larger house."

Finally, she was done arguing about it and said, "I don't like your idea. I think it's a bad decision but if you want to buy it then go ahead."

Like a child given permission to go to the park, I ran off to Lowes and made the purchase. That winter it snowed only three major times! My son and I did plow a few driveways, but the $250 we earned didn't come close

Chapter 8. Improving the Marital Foxhole

to paying it off.

Tracy was right. I was wrong. To this day when I talk about a snow thrower I still get that *"I told you so"* look from my wife. We smile wordlessly at each other because we both know that she got me. She got me good.

> **Men want respect, women want love**

When you have one of these *"I told you so"* moments in your marriage, learn and grow from them. Don't beat each other over the head with them every time a plan falls through. You'll never move forward in business, marriage – or life for that matter – if you don't take chances and live out your dreams together. Realize that you both have to make poor mistakes to grow, and expect some mistakes like this in a relationship.

Consider this: God specifically commands the husbands to *"love"* their wives, whereas wives are told to specifically to *"submit"* to their husbands.

> *"Wives, submit yourselves unto your own husbands, as it is fit in the Lord. Husbands, love your wives, and be not bitter against them."* Colossians 3:18-19.

Now, that doesn't mean that one cancels the other out; it simply reinforces the fact that men have issues with falling out of love, and women have issues with submission. In general, men want respect and women want love. Therefore the Lord laid it out simple enough for us to understand... but not to argue, fuss and fight about it with each other. If you want your marriage to be successful, put this to work and give each other what you need: love and respect.

Provide Security

Men are naturally protectors, conquerors and aggressors by design, whereas women are naturally nourishing, non-aggressive and non-confrontational. That's not to say that women can't defend themselves! Some certainly can. But in the scope of the design of the marriage, it is the husband's responsibility to provide physical security for the wife.

The 1900's Psychologist, Abraham Maslow, studied exemplary people such as Albert Einstein, Eleanor Roosevelt and the healthiest 1% of college students. Maslow summed up his studies in a graph to depicting a hierarchy of psychological needs that are fundamental requirements for survival. If these basic requirements are not met, the human body simply cannot continue to function, thus resulting in death.

Maslow's hierarchy of needs:

Self-actualization	morality, creativity, spontaneity, problem solving, lack of prejudice, acceptance of facts
Esteem	self-esteem, confidence, achievement, respect of others, respect by others
Love/Belonging	friendship, family, sexual intimacy
Safety	security of body, of employment, of resources, of morality, of the family, of health, of property
Physiological	breathing, food, water, sex, sleep, homeostasis, excretion

First is the need to survive. The metabolic needs of water, food and air are *necessary* for survival, while clothing and shelter provide protection from the environment. Breathing, eating, drinking, sleeping and excretion are the bare minimal needs that must be met before the next level of physical needs can be met – which are individual safety and security. This second level of security is broken down into categories such as personal, financial, health and well-being. Until the needs of safety and security are fulfilled, man cannot move to the third level – the emotional/social needs which are friendship, intimacy and family.

Once these needs are fulfilled, man can move forward to develop self-esteem, confidence, achievement and respect. According to Maslow's theory, once all of the other four levels of man's psychological needs are met, then man can reach his full potential and be a creative thinker, a problem-solver, and can discern facts from fiction and reality from unreality.

Chapter 8. Improving the Marital Foxhole

Long before Abraham Maslow claimed discovery, the hierarchy of needs was given in the book of Genesis beginning with Adam. Perhaps if Maslow had read and believed the Bible, it wouldn't have taken him a lifetime to develop a theory about how we come to be who we are in life and the purpose for which we were created – as found in Revelation 4:11. Regardless, I want to draw your attention to the fact that we, as spouses, have needs that must be met in marriage in order to move forward to maturity, and the husband is the primary custodian of identifying and fulfilling those needs.

> *"But if any (man) provide not for his own, and specially for those of his own house, he hath denied the faith, and is worse than an infidel."* I Timothy 5:8

When one hears the term, *"marital security"* we naturally think about financial or emotional security. However, marital security is composed of a myriad of physical, social, emotional, intellectual, occupational and spiritual dimensions.

For the purpose of this section of the book we are describing physical security provided by the husband for the wife (and, of course, the children).

Think back to the heroic movies of times past such as *King Kong, Snow White, African Queen, Gone with the Wind,* and who can forget *The Princess Bride*. Film heroes of times past such as Clark Gable, Jimmy Stewart, Humphrey Bogart, John Wayne and Clint Eastwood. In all the heroic thrillers, there's always the heroic man rescuing a distressed woman from the evil villain or savage monster.

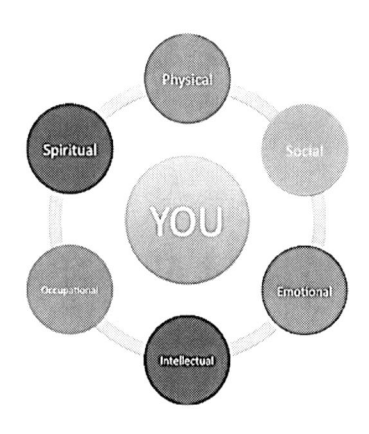

It's that type of heroic figure that husbands should try to be to their wives. Husbands, provide your wife with a blanket of psychological and physical security that she can sleep under comfortably! You may not have the karate skills of Jackie Chan, the board-chopping ability of Bruce Lee or the flying roundhouse kick of Chuck Norris. You may not have the physique of Brad Pitt or the ability to handle a .45 like Clint Eastwood....but you're still

Marriage is a Four-Letter Word

a man. So be a man and not a mouse and have a backbone and not a wishbone. As a father once said, "Be a man, boy. Stand up for your family. Let them see the hero within you."

Does that mean you may have to physically defend your family with your fists? Yes, if necessary. Could you do it if you had to? Would you freeze, fight or take flight? Realize that the most victorious fights are won with words and not fists.

Although you may never need to come to blows to protect your family, your wife and children need to know that you will defend them and be their *rescuer* in the time of need. Your children need to see you as their hero, and one that will not tolerate disrespect or disgrace to God, country or family.

> **At the age of 18, I was just as big as my father was. I was an athlete capable of defending myself. Perhaps I could've beat Dad in a fight, but I never thought to try. Not only did I have great respect for my father – he was my hero. No matter how big I got, Dad would remind me, "Son, you may be bigger than me but I'm smarter than you, and you have to sleep sometime."**

Remember a time in our not-so-distant history when boys would argue which dad was "tougher." Here's how it used to be...

Johnny, Larry and David were on the playground after school;

    Johnny: "My dad can beat up your dad."

    Larry: "Nuh-uh. My dad can beat up your dad!"

    Johnny: "Oh yeah? Well my dad can beat up Superman."

    Larry: "That's nuthin'. My dad can beat up Superman and the Green Hornet."

    Johnny: "No way. Your dad can't even beat up Mighty Mouse!"

    Larry: "Stop talkin' 'bout my dad!

Chapter 8. Improving the Marital Foxhole

> Johnny: "You stop talkin' 'bout my dad!" Johnny punches Larry. Larry tackles Johnny.
>
> Johnny and Larry roll around on the ground fighting.
>
> David breaks up the fight.
>
> Johnny and Larry shake hands and make up.
>
> Johnny and Larry remain best friends forever.

Husbands, not only should you be able to defend your family, but you should defend your country as well. Regardless of you being a member of the Armed Forces, the defense of this country goes much deeper than wearing a uniform. We no longer have to cross an ocean to fight for our country….you may have to do so in your own town.

Next time our National Anthem is played, take a look around and notice how many people don't even put their hands over their heart. They'll be on their cell phones and some will keep their hats on their heads. I'm the guy you hear shouting, "Take your hat off!"

United States Code, 36 USC Sec. 301 says that during the playing of The Star Spangled Banner (United States National Anthem) when the flag is displayed, everyone except those in uniform (military, police, etc.) should stand at attention while facing the flag and have their right hand over their heart. Individuals in attendance who aren't in uniform should remove anything they are wearing on their head with their right hand and hold it at their left shoulder, with their hand held over their heart. Individuals in uniform should show the military salute during the first note of the anthem and stay in the position until the last note. If the flag is not displayed, people in attendance should face the music and respond as if the flag were present.

Our country laws tell us to stand up, take off any hats, and place our right hand over our heart.

Americans are dropping the ball in the standards department and we, as husbands and fathers, are the gatekeepers.

This is the Pledge of Allegiance to our flag.

Marriage is a Four-Letter Word

A pledge that is no longer offered at the beginning of the day in 50% of American schools...

I pledge allegiance to the flag of the United States of America, and to the Republic for which it stands, one Nation under God, indivisible, with liberty and justice for all.

> The Pledge of Allegiance to the Flag should be rendered by standing at attention facing the flag with the right hand over the heart. When not in uniform men should remove their headdress with their right hand and hold it at their left shoulder, the hand being over the heart. Persons in uniform should remain silent, facing the flag, and render the military salute.

Men: hold others accountable and set a standard for your wives and children to know that you stand for what is right and are willing to fight for your beliefs. It's okay to take a stand. Someone, like a veteran, may thank you.

If you are a Christian, how do you respond when someone curses or uses the Lord's name in vain? Do you remain silent? Do you let it slide? If someone called your wife or mother a @!#$* would you tolerate it? Then why would you tolerate someone cursing about your Father (God and Jesus Christ)?

In restaurants: *"Excuse me guys but your language is unacceptable in this public restaurant. I have my wife and children present, and I'd appreciate it if you'd not use that language."*

Never once has it caused a fight, but when stated politely, it has always resulted in a positive outcome. Most people apologize and other around are thankful.

Once I stopped at a red light in town and noticed a guy strolling down the sidewalk.[7] He pulled the last cigarette from his pack and threw his trash on the ground. From the window of my car I yelled, "Hey! Pick up your trash."

My teenage son slumped down in the seat next to me, half-embarrassed and half-afraid that we'd be shot, yet he respected it. The guy picked up his trash. The point is that we, as citizens, have stopped holding people accountable for their action, including ourselves in our marriages.[8]

Fathers, if you choose to avoid conflict rather than hold people accountable

Chapter 8. Improving the Marital Foxhole

for their actions, you are doing your children a great disservice. If you sheepish in dealing with confrontation, then they will be able to tell. They may never come right out and tell you, but it subtracts from their sense of psychological security that you are supposed to provide.

> **I counseled with a woman whose husband was a sound sleeper – too sound to awake for an emergency. She has no confidence that he could protect her if something happened. She woke up at every little creak and moan in the house, while he would sleep through a tornado!**

All the firearms in the world will do you no good if you can't use them. You have fire extinguishers and smoke alarms, but do you discuss and rehearse a fire drill with your family? You may not be *big and strong* but does your family believe that you'll protect them? Is it "everyone for themselves," or "I'll save you honey?" Your wife and children needs to know that they are physically and psychologically secure.

Psychological Security

We spoke about physical security, which helps provide psychological (mental) security - the emotional stability that developed from peace of mind. Both husband and wife need this to live "happily ever after." The lack of this type of security will be a primary driving factor in dependence upon prescription medication (the most abused drug), disorders and/or alcohol. In counseling, I find an overwhelming majority of spouses that abuse a pill to treat a symptom, without ever treating the problem.[9]

Men derive psychological security through achieving accomplishments, which gives self-gratification. Men are tangible beings that see something, desire it, and want to conquer it. When a man is pleased with what he does and how he does it, he gains this type of psychological security. Hence, the reason a man can be very satisfied with the same routine every day. Man is a creature of habit and, in reality; it doesn't take much to please a man. Men only require the five 'S's:' Supper, Sports, Sex, Sleep and a Sense of

Marriage is a Four-Letter Word

Purpose.

Women derive psychological security intellectually. They are emotionally hardwired. They respond and react through the five senses, whereas men are primarily driven by what they see (the visual) and what they can eat. Sexually, a man can be aroused instantaneously, whereas a woman generally *warms up* and *builds up* steam.

> **"Men are like microwaves; women are like crock-pots"** [10]
> Evangelist Philip Schipper

Husbands, if you lovingly appeal to your wife's intellect and senses, she will respond! That means that you'll have to groom and bathe yourself properly. You'll have a better chance of *turning on the romance* if you smell and look presentable. Ladies, all the fruity lotions, soft music and dim candles work for you, but a man doesn't need all that stuff. They don't care if the bedroom light is on or off, or if you have one sock on and one sock off. You give an invitation and they will rise to the occasion. When things are right in a marriage – you have that power over the man.

Men are attracted by what they see. A man will walk around a new car lot for hours lusting at the new models, but most women simply wants something dependable. She don't care if it has four, six or eight cylinders. She don't care about 4WD and limited slip differential and probably doesn't know what *horsepower* and *timing chain* are. But you take that same woman and drop her off at the *Bath and Body Works* in the Mall, and you'll be waiting for a while.

Men and women are different. Thank the Lord. It's a good different! I'm glad we are different. Unfortunately, the devil knows the differences and uses that to his advantage. The reason why pornography is a 13 billion-dollar industry in the United States - because of man's attraction to the woman and the lust produced.[11]

> *"But every man is tempted, when he is drawn away of his own lust, and enticed. Then when lust hath conceived, it bringeth forth sin: and sin, when it is finished, bringeth forth death."* James 1:14-15

Chapter 8. Improving the Marital Foxhole

Every married man has received an unexpected elbow jab to the ribs when looking at something that his wife thought was inappropriate. It may happen in the shopping mall or the grocery line, but it happens. So, ladies, if you want to win your man over, let go in the bedroom and let him see you, all of you. Maintain a fit and healthy body to give your husband something good to look at and appreciate.[12] It will help keep his eyes off other women, thus improving your marital foxhole.

Sexual Security

"Marriage is honourable in all, and the bed undefiled…"
Hebrews 13:4

Keep the sexual intimacy exciting and interesting in your marriage. What you do and how you do it is between you and your spouse. Some people that I have counseled were brought up to believe that there's only one place, one method, one position… period. Some were taught that the word "sex" was a dirty word. Some were scolded if they stated the name of the human sexual anatomy, so they couldn't talk about it in the household. Many felt that the sexual relationship between the husband and wife was made to be something "dirty" and could not open themselves up to their spouse because of these feelings brought about by the way that they were raised to think or believe.

You may feel shy, naughty, intimidated or fearful to try anything new or adventurous… but what you do between the two of you is undefiled before God. If you both agree, go for it.

Don't allow you and your partner to become stuck in sexual rut. A rut is a grave with both ends kicked out, with the result being death. Don't allow your intimacy to die, because if your intimacy is no longer exciting, then you are on the road to sexual death. Communicate with each other about the things that you would like to try, especially to avoid the same old, same old. The key is to *try*. Mix it up. Avoid limiting your intimacy to the same place and position every time.

> **Discontentment and dissatisfaction breeds divorce**

A great way to facilitate excitement in intimacy is to plan a date for you and your spouse. Plan ahead with enough time to have something to look forward to on your calendar. Think young and be spontaneous. Don't allow the wear and tear of life, jobs, children and responsibilities detract from your intimacy. You have to work at keeping the love alive.

If it's been months since you've been intimate, there's a real issue there. Something is obviously wrong in your relationship. Your love for your spouse should facilitate sexual attraction and desire. If you don't have those feelings for your spouse, it will be easier for you to acquire them for someone else, which is how infidelity begins.

The deepness of love in a relationship has a direct link to the frequency of intimacy. Statistics show that happy, monogamous Christian couples have more frequent sex than anyone does. Statistics also conclude that those who frequently view pornography (primarily men) have less intimacy than those that don't view it at all.[13]

Often, sexual discontentment with a spouse is a direct result of what's being viewed. As an example, a man who views other women in magazines, movies, through pornography or Internet, burns images on his brain that affect his desires and judgment. Lust causes thoughts which are sin, and destructive to a marriage. You bring about what you think about. For a man to view another woman, and to allow himself to think about her sexually, is mental adultery.

> *"Ye have heard that it was said by them of old time, Thou shalt not commit adultery: But I say unto you, That whosoever looketh on a woman to lust after her hath committed adultery with her already in his heart."* Matthew 5:27-28

> *"...for man looketh on the outward appearance, but the LORD looketh on the heart."* 1 Samuel 16:7

Chapter 8. Improving the Marital Foxhole

Since the woman that he is lusting after is not his wife, an unregistered comparison has taken place psychologically. Over time, he can become discontented with his wife's body due to the hundreds of women that he has filed away in his mind. What you look at affects the heart!

So many wives have come to me as a counselor and discussed their hatred of the pornography that their husbands view. Competition steals the heart away. Secondly, many husbands expect their wives to do the same thing the porn stars do, which is against nature in many cases. Had they never viewed that trash, they would have nothing to compare their intimacy. If there were one major cure to establishing a deeper-connected relationship it would be in eliminating pornography.

Here's God's original intent for a husband and wife: Imagine a young man and woman that kept themselves pure until marriage. They avoided pornographic material in any way, shape or form. They never touched another boy or girl intimately or innocently.[14] They remained pure.

They wed, and on the night of their honeymoon, they uncover each other romantically for the first time, and engage in intimacy. They don't have "experience." They don't have "skills" or "tricks." Whatever they do and however they do it, they figure it out on their own. It's wonderful, it's glorious – and it's the best they have ever known! They have no former partner to compare their spouse. They have nothing positive or negative to relate to....and everything is blessed of God. That's how the Lord intended it. The bed is truly undefiled. It's pure. It's holy. Six years and two children later, they're still in love. She's changed, he's changed, yet they're still keeping the love alive.

Now consider a couple that has had numerous sexual partners in the past. They engage in a sexual relationship with each other, and eventually move in together. They have not refrained from filling their minds and bodies from sex. They shared stories and laughed at sexual jokes. They are no strangers to it.

Marriage is a Four-Letter Word

Eventually they wed, and on the night of their honeymoon intimacy is no different from before, with only the location and event changing.[15] Both of them have previous partners to compare with – and that, my friend, becomes a dangerous battlefield in the mind. The wife doesn't perform like his last girlfriend, so she compared on an invisible scale his mind. The husband doesn't please her like her second boyfriend, but she'll live with it because he makes good money. Even if one was better than the last boyfriend or girlfriend, the thoughts and images are still embedded in the brain. No big deal though, because he can handle it, right? Wrong! It's not right. Six years and two children later, she can't figure out why he doesn't want her sexually. She's changed. He's changed, and he has never been committed to her alone in mind and heart.[16] All she becomes is another woman he's in love with and the only things that has changed is a piece of paper that proclaims them married.

> **Workplace affairs are very common. Roughly half of all affairs happen at work.**[16]

Along comes some girl from the past or a woman in the workplace and he ends up leaving his wife of six years. "Wow! What happened?" What happened is they weren't sold out to each other, and he brought about what he thought about.

If you start right and stay right, you'll finish right. Teach this concept to your children and reject society's view of sexual education and protection. The only protection is abstinence for your mind, body and spirit.

> *"If we confess our sins, he is faithful and just to forgive us our sins, and to cleanse us from all unrighteousness"* 1 John 1:9

If you've filled your mind with trash, wash it with the Word and commit yourself to the Lord.

> *"Sanctify them through thy truth: thy word is truth."* John 17:7

> *"Wherewithal shall a young man cleanse his way? By taking heed thereto according to thy word."* Psalm 119:9

> *"Behold, thou desirest truth in the inward parts: and in the hidden part thou shalt make me to know wisdom. Purge me*

Chapter 8. Improving the Marital Foxhole

with hyssop, and I shall be clean: wash me, and I shall be whiter than snow." Psalm 51:6-7

... and my favorite: *"Commit thy works unto the LORD, and thy thoughts shall be established." Proverbs 16:3*

Men, when you realize what you are attracted to, it will help you avoid the devil's traps. When you realize how your wife is attracted, it should propel you to appeal to those senses. Smell good. Taste good. Look good. Sound romantic. Listen to her. Caress her. Explore her. Talk to her. Seek to please her, and you'll always please yourself in doing so.

When you appeal to her psychological needs, you credit peace of mind. A husband, who compliments his wife on how she looks, cooks and cleans increases her security, her self-esteem and her need to be an important factor of the marriage. A wife that compliments her husband on the labor he does at work, at home, and for the family increases his stock of self-worth. When you stroke his ego, you are meeting his natural desire to be your *Superman*.

When we fail to meet our spouse's emotional needs, someone else will.

Men run off with another woman who appealed to their lust primarily because they let their guard down and fell out of love:

1. They were no longer attracted to what they had at home.

2. They took their eyes off what they had at home.

3. They listened to someone that fed their ego.

4. They felt the grass appeared greener on the other side.

Women run off with and cheat primarily with someone they were close to in conversation because:

1. The man appealed to her emotional need for listening – they said pleasant things that they no longer were told at home, and they listened.

2. They appealed to her psychological need for

appreciation and security – with compliments on how they looked, how good they smelt, or how great a job they did on a project, etc.

3. They appealed to her physical need for touch – shoulder rub, a touch on the hand when expressing thoughtful conversation.
4. They appealed to her sense of smell – the smelled good.

Financial Security

Financial issues continue to be the top reason for divorce. Living beyond your financial means with a lifestyle of addictive spending habits, bills from the past, loss of income, increased child support, lawyer fees, split finances and separate bank accounts – these are all financial killers of marriages.

It is the husband's responsibility to financially provide for your family.

> *"But if any provide not for his own, and specially for those of his own house, he hath denied the faith, and is worse than an infidel."* 1 Timothy 5:8

Since the beginning of humanity, the husband has been the "breadwinner" of the family. Generally, in most countries this is true! The husband hunts, fishes, traps, farms and does whatever is necessary to take care of his family. Historically, it was socially accepted and expected that it is the man's responsibility to do so.

> **The most accurate count of stay-at-home dads was estimated at 1.4 million by Dr. Beth Latshaw in 2009. That number has likely increased to 1.75 million.**[18]

Only in America are the lines of responsibility completely blurred. Not until the 19th century did we see an ever-increasing trend in role changes within the family. Now into the 20th century, there are more stay-at-home husbands/fathers than ever before. Roles in gender are switched, with men cooking, cleaning, washing, ironing, changing diapers and taking care of the home, while more and more women are working 40-50 hours a week to pay the bills.

Chapter 8. Improving the Marital Foxhole

We are upside-down in the roles of husband and wife in America. The breakdown of the family and overall ideology of marriage causes a breakdown in roles. Parents are raising their daughters to obtain careers instead of a husband. Young men are groomed to live for themselves instead of for their wife and children. Yet God's design is for a woman to support, promote and stand behind her husband, and to maintain the affairs of the family, while the husband is to lead and guide the family by providing security (financially, psychologically, physically, etc.).

> *"The aged women likewise... That they may teach the young women to be sober, to love their husbands, to love their children, To be discreet, chaste, **keepers at home**, good, obedient to their own husbands, that the word of God be not blasphemed."* Titus 2:3-5

That doesn't mean that a woman can't work or have a career! Certainly not! But the family is first priority. I realize that the influence of society today is all about dual-income homes and equality. I got it. But doing it God's way brings peace, joy and longevity to marriage.

What I find in counseling couples is that they are so busy with their careers that they rarely have appropriate time for each other or the children. Career couples leave for work each morning, drop the kids off at daycare and school, and picking them up 10 hours later. Mommies aren't raising their children anymore – the women at Child-care do. The school does. Nannies do. Those outside influences know more about the children than some parents do.

Parents are trading their children for careers and the love of money while making excuses for their decision by saying, "I want to give my children a life I never had." Children don't know what a better, richer, or cozier life is. They don't care about that stuff... they want involvement from the parents!

I've stayed with families in third-world countries that walked on dirt for floors and the kids played with a kite made of a paper plate and a piece of yarn. They farmed together, cooked together, ate together, cleaned together, prayed together and played together. They didn't have treadmills, televisions or Tommy Hilfiger jeans. There were no computers, telephones or iPads. They probably wouldn't know what a Lego, Transformers, Hot Wheels or

Marriage is a Four-Letter Word

Barbie was even if you showed them a picture. They have nothing but each other – and that makes them completely happy.

The unique woman, wife and mother of the Book of Proverbs chapter 31 is a great example of someone who took care of her husband and household. She was a help that was suitable for her husband. She made him look good and her family praised her. She worked with her hands, she bought and sold property, the people of the city knew her, and she was very much appreciated. She was filled with wisdom, knowledge and understanding. She was well balanced with her activities. That is the woman to aspire to be.

Men, work and provide for your family. Don't force or expect your wife to pick up your responsibility to earn a living. Be the breadwinner for the family.

> *"For even when we were with you, this we commanded you, that if any would not work, neither should he eat."*
>
> 2 Thessalonians 3:10

When you provide for the needs of your wife, you will be her *knight in shining armor* that no man can steal her away. Always seek ways to improve your *marital foxhole"* and you will be better equipped to battle against all the forces that seek to tear your marriage apart.

....

In closing this chapter, I would like to leave you with three points that will get you and keep you on the right course in your marriage. They come from Ephesians chapter 5:1-2, and the simplicity is mind-blowing! If we just commit to these three things, we will be in love and produce more love than seemingly possible. Here they are….

1. Follow God (as a child does a parent).
2. Walk in love.
3. Give of yourself.

> *"Be ye therefore followers of God, as dear children; And walk in love, as Christ also hath loved us, and hath given himself for us an offering and a sacrifice to God for a sweetsmelling savour."* Ephesians 5:1-2

Chapter 9

Reasonable Rules for Raising Rug-Rats

It's only reasonable to have rules and responsibilities for children. Rules keep us accountable to one another. Rules maintain unity and order. You cannot have rules alone and expect the relationship to be self-sustaining or satisfactory. Rules alone, in absence of a good relationship, only produce rebellion.

> **"Rules without a relationship produce rebellion."**
> ~ Missionary, Dr. Humberto Gomez[1]

The following tips will assist you in managing both rules and relationships within your family.

Keep Your Bed Private

"Shared parenting bed," "family sleeping" or "co-sleeping" is actually becoming popular in some areas of the world but allowing children and pets to routinely sleep in your bed slowly separates husband and wife over time.[2]

Family bed-sharing happens slowly and unnoticeably. It begins when someone (a child) or something (a pet, a pillow, a hairdryer[3]) slowly begins to take the place of your spouse. "Just this once" for the children turns into "only on the weekends" which turns into several nights a week. I'm guilty of

Marriage is a Four-Letter Word

allowing my kids to sleep in the bed occasionally but those exceptions must be kept to a minimum.

Bed-sharing begins when the baby is brought home from the hospital and the crib is placed in the parent's room. A few months go by and the baby continues to sleep in the bedroom. More emphasis is generally placed on the baby as the parents grow distant. Many times the marital love life will slowly deteriorate due to baby distractions, feeding times, lack of sexual desire, changes in the body, etc. This is a critical time to maintain a balance between caring for the baby and caring for each other.

About the time the crib should be moved to its own room, it conveniently stays with the parents. As the baby learns to crawl and walk it ends up sleeping with the parents.

> - I counseled a couple that fought over the dog sleeping in the bed with them. She loved it but he hated it. There was no commitment or compromise, and it deteriorated their relationship so much that it affected their intimacy. They are divorced today.
>
> - One woman said that her husband's CPAP machine was ruining her sex life!
>
> - After a military deployment, I came home only to find out that I had been replaced by a body pillow. For an entire year, my wife had adjusted her sleeping habits without me, and enjoyed the comfort of a body pillow as a means of security! Imagine how I felt having been replaced by a pillow.

Any time you begin to allow someone or something else to share your marital bed, you give up a part of your intimacy that is not easily taken back. The child, object or animal you have allowed into your bedroom will expect to sleep there all the time. Unless you have the character to keep it to a minimum, the bad habit formed will continue for years, thus progressively deteriorating your relationship with your spouse. Some couples end up in separate rooms as a result.

Chapter 9. Reasonable Rules for Raising Rug Rats

To change the pattern with children, make the commitment to not make it a habit and stick with the plan. Put the children in their own beds and explain the decision. Understandably, there will be exceptions to the rule - such as being scared by a dream or a child feeling sick. That's normal but those moments should be exceptions and not the general rule.

> A nationwide study revealed that 75% of pet owners consider their pet part of their family. 48% of respondents said that their pet sleeps on the bed and hogs their covers and pillow.[4] The general need for a pet in the bed is to provide a sense of comfort, either emotional or physical (sometimes both). Adults who have this type of need lack the connection from their spouse and so the family pet fills the void.

Keep Your Bedroom Private

Your bedroom should not be the children's playground, nor your bed a trampoline. It's your private, sacred room of rest, relaxation, love and lovemaking for you and your spouse. Your privacy should be such that your children are taught to knock on your door, and ask to enter. Your most private items and weapons are usually stored in the bedroom, therefore closets and drawers should remain off limits unless consent is given. Teach your children to respect the master bedroom and it will be one of the building blocks used to teach them the intimacy of marriage as they grow older.

Don't Argue In Front of the Children

Keep your major disagreements private. Your children need to see their parents in unity, not yelling and fighting with one another. Many children grow up hearing and seeing this type of dysfunctional communication, and

Marriage is a Four-Letter Word

it's no wonder they repeat the same style of behavior as an adult.

Statistics indicate that we are a product of our genes, environment and experiences. A woman who tolerates abuse by her husband most likely tolerated some type of abuse growing up. A mother who consistently screams at her kids and husband probably picked up the trait from her upbringing. If your mom *wears the pants in the family*, then guess what you will most likely try to do? If your father talked down to you then guess what you'll have to overcome?

At some time in our lives, we've all experienced negative parental behavior and made the mental commitment, "When I grow up, I will not be like my mom/dad." Then one day, we say or do something that stops us in our tracks and we realize, "I'm just like my mom/dad!" Somewhere in the course of ancestry, we must break the mold and ensure that good habits replace the negative ones.

What are some negative habits that you should replace?

- _____
- _____

The greatest example of a marriage that your kids are exposed to is your own. They see it every day. If your marriage is a disaster, you are setting your children up for failure through your own example. Contrariwise, if you set a good example for them to follow, they will most likely exhibit those traits and carry them over into their own marriage.

What are some good examples that you want to set for your children?

- _____
- _____

If you want to stop this type of behavior, you must intentionally try some things differently than what you've ever done before. The first step to changing negative behavior of arguing in front of the children is to make a

Chapter 9. Reasonable Rules for Raising Rug Rats

commitment to take discussions that may potentially lead to an argument to the bedroom or other private area. That does not mean to fight in the bedroom! You can disagree without fighting and the children should not hear you throughout the house.

Teach your children not to argue by setting the example.

- If you tell them, "Don't argue with me" but you argue with your husband then you are setting a negative example.
- If you say, "Do what your mother said" but you don't' respect what she often says then you are setting a negative example.

By deciding not to argue in front of the children, you are training them to discuss issues logically, calmly and professionally. As they mature into young adults, teach them how they should interact when they are married by explaining the methods that you and your spouse have chosen.

Don't Argue With Your Children

I just don't get it. Why would you argue with a child? Parents who do this have lost control of who is in control. You are the parent; they are the child. You are the adult entrusted with the responsibility by God to raise them correctly. You provide food, clothing and medical attention. You make the decisions. You have the say it what happens around the house.

Any child will challenge you when they know that your word is not the final authority. When this happens, your "no" no longer means "no." It means "maybe" or it means, "If I beg mom or dad long enough, they'll change their mind."

When you allow your children to argue, fuss, fight and have the last word, you are mentoring them to react in the same manner towards their teacher, an employee, a police officer, their spouse, a supervisor and the Lord.

Marriage is a Four-Letter Word

A parent that allows their child to argue with them will have a child that whines, complains, and pitches a fit when they don't get their way. I saw a seven-year-old boy stomping, jumping up and down, and giving his mother a hard time at the grocery store. Instead of dealing with him firmly, she started counting. "One, two, three... if you don't calm down... four, five... if I get to 10 you're in trouble... six, seven." The boy wasn't fazed one little bit because he knew that he wasn't going to be in trouble."

Since when did counting ever help anyone? All counting does is give them more time to misbehave.

- "If I have to count to five..."
- "I'm not gonna' tell you again..."
- "When we get home…"
- "If you don't behave…"
- "If I have to tell you one more time…"
- "If you're good I'll buy you___..."

These types of responses don't encourage, facilitate or enforce good behavior. They are methods of bargaining and a parent should not bargain with a child.

Here are some suggestions to change this pattern:

Get back to the basics of who is in control. Talk with your spouse about what needs to be done to gain control and make commitments to make it happen – such as making a commitment not to argue or allow the child to argue. Support each other in the commitment. Fathers – you have the lead on this as the leader of the home. When a child argues with your wife, get involved and support her by stopping the disrespect in its tracks.

In dealing with teenagers, it's paramount because not only are they disrespecting their mother, but also they are disrespecting your wife! You wouldn't let anyone disrespect your wife, would you? So why allow your kids?

When the conversation leads to whining - stop it. When it leads to, "But I thought…." or, "But daddy said…" – stop it. Say, "Stop Arguing," or "Stop whining. You were told to___(clean up your room; eat your food;

Chapter 9. Reasonable Rules for Raising Rug Rats

sit down, etc.) and that's the end of it. If you continue, _____ (type of discipline) is what will happen."

When the rules are broken, follow through with the discipline that fits the *crime*. Never say, "You're grounded for a month!" if you don't fully intend to follow through with it, or if they didn't do something worth being grounded for a month! Make the punishment equal to the offense.

Ensure that Your "No" Means "No."

No doesn't mean, *Maybe*. *No* doesn't mean, "If you keep asking me then I'll give in." *No* means *No*. *Zero, zilch, nada, nay, no*. So when you tell your children "no," then don't give into them five minutes later. Remaining true to your word is a valuable character trait! It doesn't mean that you're insensitive or cruel. It means that you mean what you say.

Have you ever been stuck behind the brat in the shopping line who is tearing up the shelves and causing a fuss? Everyone watches as the mom bargains with the child. "Johnny, if you do that again you're going to get in trouble when we get home." Notice the fear of mom on little Johnny's face as he continues to whine, pout and pull candy off the shelf. There's no change. We know it, she knows it, and Johnny knows it.

"Johnny, put that back," Mom says, "Don't do that again or you're going to get it." And you're thinking to yourself, "Yeah, right lady. That's kid's not going to listen to you." What, exactly, does "it" mean? What is he going to get? A spanking? A time out? Sent to his room? Whatever "it" is, "it" hasn't done the job of changing Johnny's behavior in the past, so what makes her believe that somehow her words are going to magically change his mind now? "It" is not working.

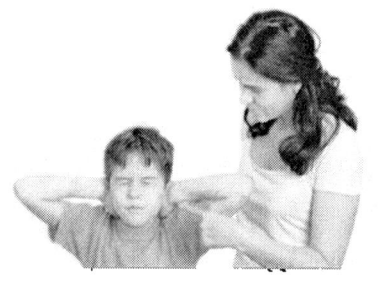

Without consistency in discipline there will be no change in behavior. Words are ignored and you can threaten all you want and it won't make a difference to a little Johnny or Suzie. Parents give in to the little Johnny

Marriage is a Four-Letter Word

and Suzy because they don't have the character to remain consistent to their word and consistent to discipline. Why? Because it takes w-o-r-k, and it takes time.

I remember long ago when Tracy and I went through a time of training our kids to stay in bed and go to sleep. We got them all ready for bed; teeth are brushed; they've gone potty; they've had their little drink. All tucked in; book was read; prayers are said; covers are snug, kisses were given and the lights turned out.

Tracy settled comfortably into bed, grabbed a book off the nightstand, opened it up and began to absorb into its pages, when all of a sudden…

"Mom?"… "Mommy?"

She looked up from the pages momentarily, and began reading again, ignoring, hoping that was the end of it. She knows that there's nothing the child needs. They've already had their drink. They have a nightlight. There's no issue. It's time for bed, and they need to go to sleep. So she continued reading.

"Mom?!"

"Go to sleep!" she said in a loud but firm voice, without looking up or even losing her spot on the page.

"But Moooooom, I need a drink of water."

"Surely they can't be serious! I'll just ignore them."

A moment passes.

"Mom, can I have a drink of water please?"

"You don't need a drink of water," she exclaims, placing the book down. "You already had a drink of water. Now go to sleep."

"But Mom… I'm thirsty."

"No. Go to sleep or get up and get it yourself," she said.

That should do it. After all, you are the boss, right?

You begin reading again…her mood for reading was all thrown off!

"Please Mom? Can I have a drink of water?"

Chapter 9. Reasonable Rules for Raising Rug Rats

At that point she slammed her book together, threw the covers back, spun out of bed and up on her feet in one-single, fluid motion. She march down the hall to the bathroom, turned on the faucet, grabbed the cup, filled it halfway with water, turned off the faucet and marched to their room. She opened the door, flipped on the light, stepped to the bed, shoved the water out to arm's length and angrily said, "Here's your water. Drink it!"

As she left the room, I heard a faint voice, "Mom, can I come sleep in your bed?"

Ugh!

Now me....I would have just ignored them, but you know how moms are. Have you ever experienced something similar?

Here are seven suggestions to create consistency:

1. Recognize and identify your inconsistencies.

2. Ask the Lord to forgive and help you.

3. Discuss the problem with your spouse and get them involved and assisting.

4. Talk to your children about it and apologize.

5. Explain the ground rules and set a course for the future.

6. Implement the plan.

7. Make corrections as needed and stick to your plan.

Next time you hear, "Mooooooom," you'll know what to do. Love but be firm. Be concerned but be consistent. Very soon, they'll get the message.

Lights Out

Getting children to bed is tough enough. Getting them to sleep with the lights off and the bedroom door closed is even tougher, but it's not an issue if you started when they are young.

Marriage is a Four-Letter Word

Children are not naturally....

- Afraid of the dark.
- Afraid of the door being closed.
- Afraid of something in the closet.
- Afraid of something under their bed.
- Afraid of the "boogeyman."
- Afraid of "monsters."

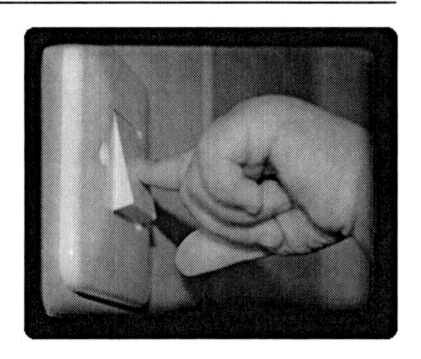

In order to be scared they must be influenced and introduced to fears such as those produced by television, movies and the certain toys.

There are two types of fear: healthy fear and unhealthy fear. Healthy fear will keep you alive. It's a respectable fear that keeps you from doing stupid things such as putting your finger on a hot stove, running from the cops or swimming with piranhas. Healthy fear will keep you out of jail and may even save your life. Unhealthy fears are abnormal and persistent phobias, such as the fear of being buried alive in a box, known as Taphephobia.[5] Or the fear of the dark - Nyctophobia, which is common in children but often passes as they mature.

Fear of the dark is not so much a fear of the absence of light as it is a fear of something that dwells in the darkness that might "leap out" or frighten unexpectedly. It's an unnatural fear that is developed by exposure to negative influences such as dad jumping out from behind the door of a dark room and scaring them, or a sibling scaring them with a fake spider.

Think about it though. We scare babies. We cover our eyes, remove them quickly and say, "BOO!" That's how fear begins. Babies aren't afraid of the dark any more than a puppy is afraid of a gun. If you stick a gun in a dog's face and he'll lick it, but if you shoot the gun beside him, he'll fear it every time he sees it.

Watch a horror movie with the sound muted. It's not scary. It's dumb. You got a big dude wearing a hockey mask and carrying a chainsaw. No big deal. The music creates the emotional drama within the psyche that produces suspense, anxiety and fear.

It makes perfect sense that a child is afraid of monsters after they've

Chapter 9. Reasonable Rules for Raising Rug Rats

watched *Monsters Inc*. It's a movie about monsters that deliver a message not to be afraid of monsters! Yeah, that really works with a three-year-old. But, hey, I was scared too after Mom took me to my first movie when I was 4 years old – *JAWS*! I'm still afraid of sharks! I remember being scared after watching movies like the *Wizard of Oz, Dracula, A Nightmare on Elm Street, Silence of the Lambs* and *the Exorcist*…and all of those movies are tame in comparison to Hollywood productions today. Movies and video games today seem much more bloody, violent, sexual and more graphic than the films of years past. Even the traditional bedtime prayer is somewhat spooky! Have you ever thought about the words?

> *"Now I lay me down to sleep, I pray the Lord my soul to keep. If I die before I wake, I pray the Lord my soul to take."*

It's no wonder kids are afraid of the dark after a prayer like that! I can hear it now… "Mommy, am I gonna die in my sleep? Will Jesus take my soul?"

"No, dear you're not going to die in your sleep, but just in case let's say this prayer…"

My firstborn, Jordan, battled fear as a little guy. To conquer his short-lived fear of the dark, I took him to a special verse in the book of Psalms, where David penned these words;

> *"What time I am afraid, I will trust in thee."* Psalms 56:3

Together we memorized this verse and the fear subsided within a few days. God works through His Word, and Jordan was given the spiritual sword to fight against fear that was not from God. Years later, Jordan still has the resources to draw upon and be victorious over fear. Even fears that are no longer the boogeyman under his bed or the dark, but fears associated with peer pressure and ridicule.

That verse still rings true for a teenager and adult, just as much as it does for a child. Adults, too, would do well to memorize this verse and use it in moments of fear, realizing that our help comes from the Lord.

> *"My help cometh from the LORD, which made heaven and earth."*
> Psalms 121:2

A humorous example of eliminating fear is demonstrated in the movie

Marriage is a Four-Letter Word

Major Payne. In this movie, a young child runs from the confines of his room afraid of the "monster" in his closet.

Major Payne marches to the boy's room, confirms the location of the monster, draws out his .45 caliber pistol and fires three rounds into the closet, thus terminating the "monster" with extreme prejudice. *"If he's still in there, he ain't happy,"* said Major Payne. The boy gives him a hug and goes back to bed. End of story. No monster, no more.

The right perspective for fear and it comes from the Word of God:

> *"For God hath not given us the spirit of fear; but of power, and of love, and of a sound mind."* 2 Timothy 1:7

Fear is a spirit and it's not of God. Help rid children of the spirit of fear by offering normalcies within your home. Don't make them afraid of the dark, but encourage them to not be afraid. Don't say things like, "The boogeyman's gonna' get you."

Show Affection

Openly confirm and reaffirm your love for your children. Shower them with hugs and kisses before they turn into teenagers when hugs and kisses are no longer cool.

Actions speak louder than words. It's easy to say "I love you" but I encourage you to show it through random acts of kindness. For example, surprise your children individually with something special. Spend time with them individually, away from the other kids, and doing something they enjoy. Watch a cartoon with them. Read them a book. Sit on the floor and play with their toys. Chase each other around the house with squirt guns. Ride bikes. Shoot hoops. Play hide-and-go-seek. It doesn't matter if

Chapter 9. Reasonable Rules for Raising Rug Rats

you are mom or dad – build those strong bonds while they're young and you'll have a connection with them when they're a teen.

Live life to the fullest and enjoy them while they are young because time flies by and soon they'll be grown and out of the house.

Take an interest in what they like – not what you like.

If your son is into snowboarding, ask him questions about it. Learn some terms such as *chicken salad*, *cross pop*, and *tailfish*.[6] Although snowboarding may not appeal to you in the least bit, by taking an active interest in something he/she enjoys, you are demonstrating your love for them and they'll KNOW it!

Fathers, take your daughter out to the shopping mall and spend time with her. She may think you've lost your mind but you will gain a relationship, and someday when she needs serious advice, she'll turn to Mom and Dad instead of her boyfriend or friends....plus she will appreciate the money you give her to spend.

If you have a good relationship with your teens and you often tell them that you love them, they will have no problem it in return. It will come naturally because your relationship will be natural.

> **Live well, laugh often, love much**

Perhaps you were raised with an absence of love. Maybe your father or mother didn't show much affection or give words of affirmation. Perhaps you rarely heard the words, "I love you" or "Good job." If that's the case, break the mold and be the father or mother you need to be to them. Don't let your past negativity influence your children. Allow yourself to show affection in the areas that you didn't receive it growing up. Allow yourself to have feelings and show your emotions for their sake and for the sake of your future grandchildren. Laugh with them, cry with them, and love them.

Affection towards spouse

Let your children see open affection and loving playfulness between you and your spouse. Share kisses and hugs in front of the children. Let them see you cuddle on the couch. Let them witness your kind acts of affection

Marriage is a Four-Letter Word

towards one another because they are learning from you. If your love has faded or drifted, take the small baby steps to bring it back to center. Get some counseling if needed and begin to do what's necessary to bring health and healing to the home.

Fathers, train your sons to honor, respect and love your wife and their mother. How they treat their mother is how they will treat their future wife. Show them what's acceptable on Mother's Day, Valentine's Day, and your wife's birthday. Show them how to keep the love alive throughout the years with flowers, cards, love notes, and open affection. Be the respectable, loveable, honorable father they can model their lives after.

Mothers, train your daughters to love, cherish and respect your husband. Show them how to take care of their future husband by setting the example. You are an open book of what to do, what not to do and how to react emotionally.

> When I was a teenager, my father would get home from work at 6 pm. Mom would begin preparing for supper at 5:30 pm so that we could eat an hour later. She developed a relaxed atmosphere for Dad to come home to. The house was clean, the beds were made, the living room was tidy, the distractions were minimal and the smell of food cooking in the oven was fabulous.
>
> I remember how refreshing it was for Dad to come home after a 12-hour work day, receive a kiss and a hug from Mom, and greeted with, "How was your day?" It was a good example of a husband and wife relationship.
>
> Years later, I get the same treatment from my wife – and you know what? It's awesome to be loved and appreciated in such a meaningful way.

Both parents play such a dynamic role in the influence of the children. The life you are leading is the life you are teaching, so make it the best life you can.

Chapter 9. Reasonable Rules for Raising Rug Rats

Vicarious

Parents often have the tendency to try to live out their dreams, hopes and aspirations vicariously through their children.

My parents encouraged me to go to college, but never demanded it. I joined the U.S. Army instead. After a few years of character building, "getting an edge on life" and "being all that I could be," I left active duty, joined the Army National Guard and started college. Had I gone to college straight out of high school, I don't think I would've had the character and definitely didn't have the desire to focus in studies and be successful. Timing is important.

Be careful about demanding that your teens grow up and follow a path that you have planned for them. Just because you graduated college and played sports doesn't mean that they will. Statistics show that young people who are forced to go to college have a lower grade point average and a higher dropout rate. There are websites dedicated to kids who are forced to go to college against their will. It increases social anxiety and places overwhelming stress upon them.

I caught part of a television show (*Toddlers and Tiaras*) about mothers who are training their toddler-daughters to be the next Miss America. They send pictures in to modeling agencies, hoping to be the next cute face in a magazine. They spend thousands of dollars in preparing their daughters for the runway, entering them into pageants, parading them on stage and making a show out of something their daughter could care less about. Then they get upset when their child doesn't win!

Many dads are no better. Take sports, for example. Some fathers place extreme pressure on their kids to play certain sports, thereby turning them into that hopeful, professional athlete.

Marriage is a Four-Letter Word

As I wrote this original portion of the chapter I was on deployment in Afghanistan. I was able to call home and caught my wife at my son's first t-ball practice. How exciting for my six-year-old boy! He had his new baseball glove, his team t-shirt on, new cleats on his feet, and he was the only child out there with baseball pants. Izak felt like he was a real baseball player, and I was proud of him![7]

> "It's funny," Tracy said, "Every other kid is wearing shorts but Izak has his cute little baseball pants on and he thinks he's the man." A smile came across my face as I held the phone up to my ear. "That's my boy!" I stated. "He may not know how to play yet but he looks like a baseball player! When is his first game?"

> "Well, this is both a game and practice," she said. "They do both at the same time."

> "That's crazy. Why would you do both at the same time? You gotta' have a practice before the real deal." I said. "That's dumb. What's the score?"

> "They don't keep score," she said.

> "What?" I exclaimed, "You've got to be kidding me! What do you mean they don't keep score? What kind of sissy team is he playing on?" I asked. "How will they know who wins?"

> "I don't know. They just kinda' do their own thing. They don't even have positions on the field. The coach just tells them to pick wherever they want to go, and Izak looks for a spot where nobody else is. Last inning he tried to play 2nd base but another girl on the team beat him to it, so he went to the outfield," Tracy said.

> "Izak let a girl take his position?" I joked. "I can't believe this. How soft has society become that they don't even keep score because they probably don't want to hurt kids' self-esteem! What's the sense of playing if you don't keep score and learn positions? How will they know who won? How will they understand the thrill of victory or the agony of defeat? How will they know the fundamentals of the game? Somebody's always a winner and someone's always a loser" I expressed."

I guess things have changed over time. I've coached basketball, volleyball

Chapter 9. Reasonable Rules for Raising Rug Rats

and football... and I had never experienced this before! I just wasn't prepared to hear of it happening on a team that one of my sons plays! If I would've know that information, we would've found a different league for Izak.

"He's up to bat," she said.

My heart began to beat for Izak. "Please Izak. Keep your shoulder squared, bat level, hit it firm, swing all the way through and get on base," I pleaded inside.

"Uh-oh, I think he's hitting the wrong way. The coach is changing Izak's grip. Looks like he's holding the bat wrong. Does he hit right or left-handed?" she asked.

"He hits left-handed!" I shouted into the phone nearly in a state of panic. "Is his left side to the pitcher or his right side?" I asked.

"His left side," she stated calmly.

"Tracy, tell the coach he's left-handed! Don't let him hit right handed," I said.

Tracy replied, "Well, he actually does pretty good hitting that way. You know, the other day he...."

"Tracy! Tell the coach to switch him to the other side of the plate!" I said anxiously. I could faintly hear that they were still trying to get Izak set up in the batter's box.

"Coach! Coach!" she shouted, "Coach, he's left-handed. Izak's left-handed."

I could hear the coach say something back but couldn't make out the words.

"Did he switch him?" I asked

"Yes, they switched him," she said.

"Which side of Izak is facing the pitcher now? Left or right?" I asked just to be sure. "His right side," she said.

"Whew. Good!" I said. "Sorry to be like that, but do you know why it's important to me?"

Marriage is a Four-Letter Word

"No. Not really," she said.

"Izak is left handed and has an advantage in sports. He needs to bat left-handed." I said. You could sense my overbearing athletic side coming out – the one-time-athlete and part-time-coach within me was giving her lessons that she couldn't care less about.

"Yeah. Well okay," she said. "They switched him and he's ready to bat."

I'm sure Tracy was thinking – It's not a big deal! Calm down Brian. They switched him and it will be all right.

> **Less than 10% of athletes are left-handed, which means that 90% or more are right-handed and are used to playing against right-handed batters, dribblers, pitchers, and kickers.**

Perhaps I also have unspoken dreams of my kids becoming the super athlete that I never was.

Therein holds one of the gems that I am trying to give in this portion of the chapter. As I was all stressed out about how my boys was hitting the ball, Tracy was kicked back and enjoying the game from the bleachers. It didn't matter to her if Izak hit left-handed or right-handed. It didn't matter if he played outfield of first base. It didn't matter if he got on base or got out… as long as he was having fun and enjoying the game. God used this story to help me understand that the things we sometimes put great emphasis on really don't matter in the scope of things.

Many parents who want to see their children succeed become over-zealous in their support. As a coach, I have experienced parents arguing and fighting in the bleachers. I've seen parents yell and scream at their kid when they missed a shot, fumbled the ball, or stepped out of bounds. It's okay if the coach yells and shouts a few commands, but it's unacceptable when parents go off on their kids who are simply trying to do the best they can. As parents with good intention, allow your kids to have fun and enjoy the game.

During the first season of high-school football I expressed to my eldest son, Jordan,

"Son, you have one shot at playing high school football. You'll

Chapter 9. Reasonable Rules for Raising Rug Rats

never get the opportunity to do it again. There are no do-overs, no replays, no second chances, and no rewinds in life. Once it's over - it's over. You can't get back what you missed so live each play to make a positive memory.

For the rest of your life you will look back and remember the years you played the game. The intensity in which you played will be remembered. There can be no regrets. Don't hold back and don't sell yourself short because of an ache, a pain or shortness of breath. You can rest when the gamer is over.

Son, I want you to go out there and do the very best you can. I will not be disappointed in you if you give it your all! You are Hurricane Hargis. You're a lean, mean, quarterback-sacking machine. You're the roughest, toughest, meanest, fiercest eighth grader ever to play the game of football. So get your oversized pads out on the field and kick some butt! One hundred percent! And most of all, son, above all else, have fun. Enjoy the game. Enjoy your youth."

Forcing a Square Peg into a Round Hole

It's proper for parents to influence, train and guide children along into fields of opportunities, but understand that your children have a different personality than you do. You like mushrooms, they like carrots. You enjoy Facebook, and they enjoy Snap Chat. You like Nike, and they like UnderArmour. You enjoy basketball and they like swimming. You like classical music, they like contemporary. You like the guitar, they like the drums. You play golf, and they think it's boring.

You like to shoot guns, and they would rather go shopping. You still use a Blackberry and they want the new iPhone 12z. Different doesn't mean "wrong," it simply means different.

Marriage is a Four-Letter Word

> **Different doesn't mean it's wrong… it simply means different.**

If you want to have a close relationship with your kids, especially your teens, then allow your kids to be kids and help them develop their own identities, desires, likes and dislikes. Enjoy them while they are young and be involved in their developmental growth! Teach them to enjoy the life and talents that God gave them, even if they are different from yours.

> *"Every good gift and every perfect gift is from above, and cometh down from the Father of lights, with whom is no variableness, neither shadow of turning."* James 1:17

If your daughter wants to try out for T-ball instead of the school Spelling Bee, allow her. If your son wants to play in the music band instead of playing football, encourage him. If your teen wants to be a Junior Usher or sing in the choir, enable them.

Don't try to force them into your one-size-cookie-cutter mold because it may only backfire on you, leaving a trail of resentment and strife.

When Jordan was 14, he told me that he wanted to learn how to play the electric guitar! The electric guitar? What, do you want to be in some big-hair rock-n-roll band? Why not start out with just an acoustic guitar? But he was adamant. "No dad he said, "It's not like that. I just really want to learn how to play the electric guitar." So we bought him an electric guitar, a small amp, and lessons for a year. Jordan now leads the church congregation in worship songs using both the electric and acoustic guitar. He is a talented musician that is a blessing to all that hear him.[8]

When Izak was 10, he told us that he wanted to learn how to play the piano. "The piano?! Why not the electric guitar like your brother?" I remarked. "Dad," said Izak, "I don't want to learn how to play the guitar. I like the piano." So we bought him a piano and he's currently taking lessons and doing great!

Chapter 9. Reasonable Rules for Raising Rug Rats

Just recently, Levi, my youngest son, told me, "Dad, I want to learn how to play the drums." "The drums?!" I exclaimed, "Are you out of your mind? Why can't you learn how to play the guitar or the piano like your brothers?"

Now I'm off to purchase a set of drums that will drive Tracy and me crazy.

....

> Ritchie Moody,[9] a close friend of mine, was a superb left-handed baseball pitcher for Oklahoma State University. Ritchie pitched the college world series in 1991 and was drafted by the Texas Rangers during an era when Nolan Ryan was still throwing' 96 mph fastballs![10]
>
> Several years and a few shoulder surgeries later, he was forced to retire from his professional career and moved back to his home state of Ohio where he began to coach baseball and develop a business to develop and train athletes.
>
> As his son grew up, Ritchie naturally steered him towards baseball. Baseball, baseball, baseball. It was eat, drink, and sleep baseball. However, the day came when his son quit baseball. It just wasn't something that interested him any longer.
>
> Shortly thereafter, Ritchie and I were shooting hoops in his driveway and he opened up to me privately about his feelings. "How could my son not want to play baseball?" He remarked. I could sense the hurt in his voice. "He's always played baseball," he said. "Ritchie," I told him, "You gotta' let him go. You can't force him to play baseball when his heart's not in it. He's not you. Let him figure things out on his own and he'll probably come back around."
>
> A few years passed, and his son matured into a teen and decided to play baseball – all on his own. Amazingly, the kid came back strong but his eager passion still wasn't baseball. He found that he could rock a guitar and had amazing talents in other things.

The moral of this section is this: be careful trying to force your children to be what you did or didn't become. Don't try to make them the super athlete, soldier, model, doctor, lawyer or preacher you were or weren't. They have their own ideas, dreams and desires, so let them choose on their own. Encourage them for the right things, guide them, lead them, mentor them and give them a nudge every now and then… but don't force them. If you do, they may rebel.

Negative Influence

Parents are the worst at encouraging kids to do wrong. Parents getting drunk and stupid, and fighting with each other in front of the kids. Parents arguing and cursing at each other, and expecting the kids not to act the same way. Moms allowing their daughters to dress like prostitutes, and arguing with dad about how they dress. At a time when I didn't think that shorts could get any shorter, I saw a group of teen girls at a middle school wrestling match with shorts much shorter than Daisy Dukes of Hazard County, with words across the derriere such as *hottie, cuttie, booty camp, pink and luscious*. What in the world? You're gonna' put a sign on your butt and expect that people won't look at it? You are advertising your body and parents are allowing it.

What has our society come to? It's no wonder that families are in the messes that they are. Values, constraints and limitations are gone out the window. Moms are enabling their daughters to flaunt their bodies and dads are encouraging their sons to sow their wild oats "but don't get her pregnant!"

> *"Train up a child in the way he should go: and when he is old, he will not depart from it."* Proverbs 22:6

This Bible promise works like a two-edged sword. It's both a promise and a curse. If you train them up in the right way – the Biblical ways of the Word – you have just as much of a promise as when you train them up in the wrong way – the unbiblical ways of the world.[11]

Moms and dads – you are training your children in one of those two ways. All your words, actions and examples are saying, "This is the way to go." You are pointing them in either a right or wrong direction. One thing is for sure…..they will follow your example. So what direction are you leading them?

Chapter 9. Reasonable Rules for Raising Rug Rats

> **"What you do in moderation, your children will do in excess."**
> ~ Dr. Jack Patterson[12]

You are the parent, the adult – and they are the children. Set boundaries according to God and give them great examples to follow.

> *"Children, obey your parents in all things: for this is well pleasing unto the Lord."* Colossians 3:20

Mom said that I was a strong-willed kid but I don't recall her saying, "I can't get Brian out of bed." Do you know why? She had two very effective methods of getting me up on those summer mornings:

1. The broom.
2. Dad.

Which do you think I had the most respect? I'll give you a hint...it wasn't the broom. You see, my father was an active participant in molding my behavior, and my mom used this tool to her advantage. They worked together without compromise. All Mom had to say was, "Do you want me to tell your father when he gets home?" That would pretty much solve any rebellion issues.

In counseling, I often have parents remark, "I can't get my son to do _____" or, "My daughter won't do_____" Or, "My two year old won't sit down." I cringe inside. The answer to solving the problem is simple, but the work involved is complex. It takes consistency.

What you do in moderation your children will do in excess. So if you let walk all over you and talk back to you, how will they raise their own kids? Fathers, husbands – take the lead on being consistent and expecting consistency in discipline. A verse describing the attributes of a good father shows that he has good leadership and his children obey....

> *"One that ruleth well his own house, having his children in subjection with all gravity;"* 1 Timothy 3:4

We can benefit from this verse both doctrinally and spiritually by applying it to our own lives. Let your wife and children see Christ in you. Be a good, positive example, lead with love, enforce discipline and your family will generally follow in submission.

So many kids are growing into adults and leaving church behind. They haven't experienced the real relationship with God. They've seen religion, and for many, it's been fake in the home. Children realize it's fake when they fail to see their parents experience a real relationship with God. Any relationship that might have been there was clouded by inconsistency and hypocrisy. All the rules, regulations, and a bunch of talk about a wonderful God was for nothing. I've been told, "Preacher, if God is so wonderful, then how come our home was like Hell growing up. Sure, we went to church but it sure didn't follow us home."

It makes perfect sense that they would leave the church and God behind. Yes, it's still an excuse, but it attest to the problem - parents are contributing to the negative influences that mold children into who they are as adults. We must recognize those negative traits and eliminate them with God's help.[13]

Play Often

A young child's mind thinks in simplistic terms of eating, sleeping and playing. Some adults never grow out of that mindset. They know more about playing than they do about working, and so their life becomes unbalanced.[14]

> *"A false balance is abomination to the LORD: but a just weight is his delight."* Proverbs 11:1

My grandparents come from an era of hardworking people. Both were raised on farms in the 1920s, and both know what it was like to wake before the sun rose, tend to chores feeding farm animals and milking cows before breakfast… only to walk to school, walk home and tend to more chores, eat supper and go to bed before sunset. That was American life back then.

Chapter 9. Reasonable Rules for Raising Rug Rats

People lived shorter lives, work was more physical…but marriages, relationships, and handshake promises were stronger.

Grandpa was a WWII Veteran of the Omaha Beach invasion of Normandy, France on June 6, 1944. Grandma went to work in a factory, as so many of the women did.[15] After the war they married and moved to Dayton, Ohio where Grandpa found work in the production plant of General Motors. Both were faithful to church, faithful to work, faithful to each other and faithful to their children.

Grandpa's hardworking traits were passed down to my father who continues to work 50-60 hours a week as a machinist. He's faithful to church, faithful to work, faithful to mom and faithful to me, his son, just like Grandpa was faithful to him.

Both Dad and Grandpa were never one for much play. They come from long lines of hard work to support their families and simply survive, so when Grandpa was growing up, there wasn't much time for play because of all the work that needed to be done around the farm. The saying was "Idle hands are the devil's workshop."

Dad's generation of the late 50s and 60s was much different, yet he still realized the importance of commitment to work in order to financially provide food and a home for the family. In my youth of the 70s and 80s, the decline of the working class in society was evident. Both government assistance (welfare) and divorce increased dramatically. Now, in my children's generation, the 20th century, there are more divorces, more cohabitation, more on welfare, more on disability, and more unemployment than in the entire history of our country. In just four generations, the evidence of social ruin is obvious. It's hard to imagine where we will be in another 20 years if the Lord's return is later than expected.[16]

I said all that to say this: Grandpa didn't play much. He was a die-hard worker that fiddled around outside and in the garage in his free time. It seemed like he was always working on some project in the garage or garden.

Dad developed the characteristics of Grandpa. He's was a hard worker and, although he made more time than Grandpa did, it was limited because of his heavy workload. Don't get me wrong, I wasn't deprived and my father loved me very much, yet we never rode a roller coaster, went for a jog or played

Marriage is a Four-Letter Word

Atari together…but the one thing that I can recall are the numerous bike rides together, which was something dad enjoyed. Those are the playful memories of spending quality time with dad.

I never saw a professional sporting game with Dad. We never went ice-skating, rollerblading, roller-skating or swimming together. But we did go to car shows, gun shows, fishing, to the Air Force Museum.

Both Grandpa and Dad are heroes of my life. From them I learned the valuable lessons of what it means to spend quality time with my children. I try the things that they enjoy doing – those things that I may not feel comfortable with - but I do it any ways. It's those memories that they will remember.

....

As I finish the chapter I'm in Afghanistan again, separated from the ones I love the most. I've missed six Christmases, nine anniversaries and birthdays too many to count. Though it all, I realize what is important in life:

1. God
2. Family.

When this life comes to a close and death is knocking at the door, what will matter is not what most people think. It's won't be the late hours at the office, the money or the paycheck. It won't be the houses that you own, the SUV you drive, the business you built or the garden you grew. It won't be in the certificates on the wall or the trophies on the shelf. It won't be how awesome of a Green Beret, doctor, teacher, coach or preacher that you were.

But it will be about the people to your left and right…..family and the relationship with the almighty God above. That's what will matter.

> *"Let us hear the conclusion of the whole matter: Fear God, and keep his commandments: for this is the whole duty of man."* Ecclesiastes 12:13

I received a Father's Day card from my six-year-old Levi and it said, "What's a dad?" (There's a picture of a dog with a ball in its

DAD

He can play like a kid, give advice like a friend, and protect like a body guard

mouth). Open the card and it reads, "He's a grownup who never forgot how to play!"

Your kids will love you when you spend quality time with them. Play the silly, stupid games that they like. Do the things that are uncomfortable to you to make them happy – such as sleeping in a tent or playing family kick-ball.

If you do that, it won't be a matter of making time for them anymore – it will become normal life for you.

> **Take an interest in what your children are interested in, and your children will be interested in you.**

When work is done, come home and play hard. When church is over, leave and spend time with your family. Turn off the TV, computer and video games and iPhones and put a puzzle together, color a picture, play Monopoly and wrestle with them. Your *mommy or daddy points* to them will skyrocket in their minds.

Life should not be dull, boring and lifeless. Your life should be full of enjoyment with your children, full of God, and full of joy.

Boys Need a Man

There are some things that my boys are better at than I am. Take skateboarding, for example. Once on vacation I tried to skateboard down a ramp and about killed myself. I admit that I have no skateboard skills (or *skilz* as they would spell it), but my kids do. My oldest son has this skateboard-looking gizmo on two wheels called a Rip Stick. He's really good at it. I can't get three feet without falling off it and twisting my ankle, and so we laugh

Marriage is a Four-Letter Word

and joke about it. He knows I'll never be Tony Hawk but he likes that I take an interest in something he enjoys.[17]

Be the father for your children that they can have upmost confidence. You may not be any good at basketball, but at least shoot hoops with them. They may beat you at checkers, but at least play and enjoy it with them. Not only will it create strong bonds between you, it will strengthen them psychologically in their perception of what and who you are.

There may come the day when my children run faster than me, are stronger than me, taller than me, and in many ways, smarter than me. I accept that. Children, especially boys, need to see their dad as the hero of the family and the role model of their life.

Far too many children no longer want to grow up and "be just like my dad," and too many fathers don't want their children to grow up and be like them either! One out of every three children in America grows up without a consistent father figure in their life. They don't have a male role to influence them directly and daily. Their role models become Irvin Iverson, Kid Rock and Tony Hawk, and so there is a noticeable disconnect in the men's department.

Men – be a man. Be hard. Be stern. Be approachable. Be fair. Be loving, patient, kind, and merciful. Be their protector. Most of all – BE THERE.

> **A father was conducting business on the computer and his son came and asked, "Daddy, may I ask you a question?" Father said, "Yeah sure, what it is?" So his son asked, "Dad, how much do you make an hour?" Father got bit upset and said, "That's none of your business. Why do you ask such a thing?" Son said, "I just want to know. Please tell me, how much do you make an hour?" So, father told him "I make $20 an hour."**
>
> **"Oh", the little boy replied, with his head down. Looking up, he said, "Dad, may I please borrow $5?" The father furiously said, "If the only reason you asked about my pay is so that you can borrow some money to buy a silly toy or other nonsense, then march yourself to your room and go to bed. Think why you are being so selfish. I work hard every day and don't have time for this nonsense."**

Chapter 9. Reasonable Rules for Raising Rug Rats

The little boy quietly went to his room and shut the door. The father sat down and started to get even angrier about the little boy's questions. How dare he ask such questions only to get some money? After about an hour or so, the father had calmed down, and started to think, "May be there was something he really needed to buy with that $5." The father went to the door of little boy's room and opened the door. "Are you a sleep, son?" He asked. "No daddy, I'm awake," replied the boy. "I've been thinking, maybe I was too hard on you earlier. It's been a long day and I took out my aggravation on you. Here's the $5 you asked for."

The little boy sat straight up, smiling "Oh thank you dad!" He yelled. Then, reaching under his pillow he pulled some crippled up dollars. The father, seeing that the boy already had money, started to get angry again. The little boy slowly counted out his money, then looked up at his father.

"Why do you want money if you already had some?" the father grumbled. "Because I didn't have enough, but now I do," the little boy replied. "Daddy I have $20 now. Can I buy an hour of your time? Please come home early tomorrow. I would like to have dinner with you."

~ For Ministry Workers ~

Allow your Children to Experience the Joy of Ministry

Caution for those in the ministry – Don't sacrifice your family while you win the world for Jesus. Far too many men of God attempt to reach the world with the Gospel while their family went to *Hell*. God is not pleased with this type of imbalance. God entrusted you with a family and it's your responsibility to provide for them physically, mentally, emotionally and spiritually.

> *"But if any provide not for his own, and specially for those of his own house, he hath denied the faith, and is worse than an infidel."*
> I Timothy 5:8

> **"If you're not having fun as a Christian, you're not doing it right!"**
> ~ Evangelist David Spurgeon[18]

Too often, ministers bring the negative side of the ministry home to the family, and over time, they wonder why their family never wants to be a part of the ministry.[19]

Family members should see the joy of you serving the Lord and the excitement that it is to be a part of the Lord's ministry. Yes, there are ups and downs in ministry. Any time you deal with people, you deal with problems. Any time you deal with problems, it can be stressful and depressing, but your family needs to see the upsides of the Lord's work and not all the downsides associated with it. If all your children ever recognize in your life is the grief associated with the ministry, what would compel them to want to be in the ministry?

> *There may be troubles and trials in this life, but you can't beat the saved life!*[20]

The saved, Christian life is the best life! That's what we need to focus on in ministry!

> **"The door to the room of success swings on the hinges of opposition."** ~ Dr. Bob Jones Sr.

I sit back in amazement and thankfulness that God would even use me in the ministry, yet He does. I want to pinch myself to see if it's real sometimes. I say, "God, you are too cool. You are awesome." Thankfulness is what you should bring out to your family. Sure, the ministry is not all great testimonies of blessings and grace (not with humans involved!). It's not all a bed of roses… but success is not measured in terms of wealth or the lack of problems. Success for God's ministry cannot be measured in attendance and offerings. Success for the Christian is to know the will of God for your life, and do it!

If you have lost that vision and care for your family, revive it. When ministry becomes a career, an everyday job, or downright drudgery, then it's time to step back, re-evaluate, step down or step away as the Lord

Chapter 9. Reasonable Rules for Raising Rug Rats

directs.

If the ministry no longer gives you joy, then your joy-maker is broken. As one preacher said in an old-fashioned Camp Meeting Revival service, "Get under the spout where the blessings come out and then you can shout!"

As you labor in the ministry, allow your kids share in serving the Lord so that they can see His goodness in it. God is awesome, and His work is great. Serving Him in a full-time capacity is the most rewarding experience on the face of this planet and your children need to know it. What better way for them to know than for them to see it in you? They should see the joy bells of service ringing inside you.

Let them see you talk to God, worship God and praise God. Let them see you in love with God… not only in the church sanctuary, but also in your everyday life. Let them see you bless the Lord when your transmission goes out and you're late for a meeting. Let them see the God of the valleys as well as the mountains. If you only praise him at church, then you're kids won't praise him at all.

> *"For a day in thy courts is better than a thousand. I had rather be a doorkeeper in the house of my God, than to dwell in the tents of wickedness."* Psalms 84:10

As a youth minister I was speaking to a PK (preacher's kid) about following in his father's footsteps on the mission field. I asked, "Are you going to serve the Lord on the mission field like your dad?" He replied, "No way! I don't want all those problems that my dad has. It's misery."

The PK was exposed to all the grief and labor of ministry, but not the joy of ministry. He saw the ministry as burdensome, rather than burden-lifting. Needless to say, the young man is not serving the Lord today.

Marriage is a Four-Letter Word

Lastly, avoid introducing your wife to your problems in the ministry. She may be your best friend, but she is not designed to bear the load that God has entrusted you. She is an emotional creation of God and unnecessarily burdening her with ministry cares will eventually lead to problems. Lovingly confide in and communicate with her about the necessary issues, but choose carefully how much you place upon her.

God entrusted you with the ministry, not to her. God called you to be the ordained minister, not her. She's there to assist and help you, not be a co-laborer of the burdens.

> *"Likewise, ye husbands, dwell with them according to knowledge, giving honour unto the wife, as unto the weaker vessel."* I Peter 3:7

Develop a good go-to friend in ministry. That's the person with whom you can share the burdens and struggles. Then you'll have two confidants – the Lord and another man.

> *"Casting all your care upon him; for he careth for you."*
>
> 1 Peter 5:7

Chapter 10

Forgive and Forget

Forgiving and forgetting are two of the most difficult challenges within a marriage. Forgiveness requires a willingness to look past your spouse's faults and replace bitterness with love. Forgetting is a process that takes time! The more you love, the easier it is to be hurt, yet the more you love the easier it is to allow those bad memories to fade away.

Forgiving

Forgiveness doesn't mean that you condone the action as if it never happened. For the spouse who lies, commits adultery, runs up gambling debt, gets thrown in jail for a DUI, or punches holes in walls when angry….forgiveness is possible but that doesn't give the spouse a free ticket to repeat the action. No, there are certainly consequences and repercussions for what they have done. Forgiving them simply means that you allow love to overshadow the wrong, and put things into perspective so that your spouse can work on the issues necessary to propel you both forward into your future.

Many find it easy to forgive the little wrongs, while holding larger issues in content for days, weeks, months and even years. This is a type of selective forgiveness that places your spouse under bondage of the *"if"* factor.

Marriage is a Four-Letter Word

- "I'll forgive you *IF* I see a change in you."
- "I forgive you, but *IF* you ever do that again…"
- "I forgive you only *IF* you…"

Sincere and true forgiveness comes from real love, and real love comes from God because He is love.[1] The more of God you have in you, that is, the closer of a relationship you have with Him, the easier it is to forgive others that do you wrong.

> **More of God filling you equals more forgiveness that you have to give.**

The word "*forgive*" is found 56 times in the Bible, whereas the word "*forget*" is found 54 times. "*Forgiving*" is found four times, whereas "*forgetting*" is only found once. Jesus used the word "*forgive*" twenty times in Scripture, and never once used the word "*forget*."

Okay, so what's all that mean?

It means that sincere forgiveness looks past the pain and loves the person despite who they are and what they do. When you humble yourself and exalt your spouse, you are in second place. It's easier to forgive when you're not #1! And so when you love your brother, father, mother, son, daughter and neighbor more than yourself, it's easier to forgive them also.

> *"Let nothing be done through strife or vainglory; but in lowliness of mind **let each esteem other better than themselves.**"*
> Philippians 2:3

> *" … Thou shalt love thy neighbour as thyself. There is none other commandment greater than these."*
> Mark 12:31

With this type of mindset, you'll be able to forgive someone without even knowing what they've done or how severe it was.

Susan: "Did you hear what she said about you?"

Jeff: "It doesn't matter. I forgive them."

Susan: "How can you forgive them when you don't even know what they did?"

Chapter 10. Forgive and Forget

Jeff: "Because we all make mistakes, and they probably don't realize what they are doing."

Susan: "Yeah, but she said that..."

Jeff: "I really don't want to hear it. It's not worth my time and effort. I forgive them. That's that."

Do you remember what Jesus said to Apostle Peter on the subject of forgiveness?

> *"Then came Peter to him, and said, Lord, how oft shall my brother sin against me, and I forgive him? till seven times? Jesus saith unto him, I say not unto thee, Until seven times: but, Until seventy times seven."* Matthew 18:21-22

He told Peter to forgive 490 times. What exactly did Jesus mean? I mean, after all, Peter asked an honest and reasonable question! Seven times to forgive is more forgiveness than the average person can muster. We write people off after the first or second time, sometimes chalking it up as "tough love." But three times? Three times is the limit Lord![2] Yet Jesus' comeback is mind-blowing, mind-numbing, mind-boggling," *I say not unto thee, Until seven times: but, Until seventy times seven."*

Did Jesus mean that after 490 acts of forgiveness you are released forever from forgiving again? Not quite. You see, if you can forgive someone 490 times... then you'll have no problem forgiving them 491, 492, 493, 494 and so forth.

Jesus shows us that with a clean heart as unto himself, you can forgive no matter how hard someone stomps you into the ground.

Now check this out...

Forgiveness doesn't mean continued toleration. You don't have to let people walk all over you. You can forgive someone and still distance yourself.

Marriage is a Four-Letter Word

> **Phyllis is a dear friend and Chaplain to female inmates. Her daughter has been in and out of jail and drug rehabilitation. She has repeatedly lied and stolen from her, and, unfortunately, she has used, abused and refused her mother's love.**
>
> **After many years of pain and anguish because of her daughter's choices, Phyllis chose to stop bailing her daughter out of trouble and attempting to turn her around. Phyllis loves her daughter and even forgives her daughter for all the wrong, however, she cannot continue to put herself in the position to be walked on and taken advantage of. The pain is too much to bear, and it is only the Lord that can turn her daughter around. This is called tough love.**

In 1998, my wife was robbed and assaulted in downtown Dayton, Ohio. She was walking into her office building on a sunny Saturday morning when the assailant grabbed hold of her and proceeded to punch her in the face while demanding money.

When he realized that she didn't have any money, he dragged her to the car and forced her to unlock the door in an attempt to kidnap her, perhaps to take her to an ATM. By a miracle of God, another employee pulled into the parking lot and witnessed the assailant holding Tracy at the car. She hit the gas, honked her horn and attempted to run him over with her SUV. The assailant fled.

The second miracle was that a bicycle patrolman (Officer Chris Fischer, DPD) heard the squeal of the tires and the honking of the horn. He pedaled around the corner and saw the women in distress. After calling for backup, they chased down and arrested the criminal nearly a mile away.

Tracy was cared for and taken to the police station for testimony where she was able to call me. How do you think I reacted? I wasn't calm, cool or collected. I wanted to kill that 19 year-old punk. My wife's face was black and blue, and for the next year, she couldn't be in the same room with a young black man with hair in cornrows because of PTSD.

In the subsequent court proceedings, *M. Gibson* was convicted of assault and robbery and was sentenced to six years in prison. He was in an Ohio State

Chapter 10. Forgive and Forget

prison, and so was I with all the anger, bitterness and resentment. It took nearly three years for the Lord to do the work in my heart.

Today, I would like to sit across the table from her attacker and say,

> "Gibson, I hate what you did. You hurt the person I love the most in life. You damaged her face with your fist. You robbed her of peace and security for many years. Your actions were selfish and devastating. You did the crime and you did the time with six years in prison. According to the State of Ohio, you have paid your debt to my wife and society.
>
> Gibson, what you did was horrible, but I love you enough as a person to see you come to Jesus Christ. I have forgiven you and I pray that you have asked Christ to forgive you, as well as forgiven yourself."

You see, God performed an operation of love in my heart...a love for the sinner. He taught me a lesson about forgiving and forgetting by using the devastating circumstance to create the Self-Defense Combat Course that has trained numerous men, women, boys, girls and military personnel since 2001.[3]

....

The Bible proclaims Jesus Christ as the greatest example of forgiveness. As He hung from the nails that protruded though His hands and feet fastening Him to a rugged cross; as He bled from His whipped, ripped flesh and beaten face; as He received an onslaught of mocking remarks from the Messiah-rejecting crowd.....Jesus looked down from the cross and made this astonishing request to His father above: "Father, forgive them for they know not what they do."[4]

Our Jesus hates sin, but He loves the sinner enough to save each and every one.[5] He is not willing that any should perish, but that all should come to repentance. It's with that kind of love that Jesus forgives us for a lifetime of sin, and continues to forgive when we stumble and fall throughout life's journey.

What obstacles have you overcome in your life? What addictions have you

Marriage is a Four-Letter Word

been given victory over? What have you been forgiven of? Take a moment to focus on all the things that God has forgiven you of – including those things done in secret that nobody else knows about. When you asked the Lord to forgive you, He never failed to extend His forgiveness or His awesome mercy. He loves you!

For many of us that spent a long time developing bad habits, it sometimes takes a long time to achieve victory. Yet time and time again we get up, brush off and ask for forgiveness and move forward with his help.[6] Even after failing and trying again, did He ever stop forgiving? No. Not even after the 100th failure. He understands that we are frail.[7] He wants us to keep at it. Yes, sometimes there is discipline when we sin willfully.[8] Discipline and consequences do not mean that His forgiveness has run out. Thankfully it never does. It comes because He loves us and (like good parents) wants us to turn out right.

Terry Caffey is a long-distance friend in Texas who awoke at 3:00 a.m. on March 1, 2008 to find his daughter's boyfriend standing in his bedroom with a gun. He opened fire, killing Terry's wife, his two sons, and wounding him 12 times, before setting the house ablaze.

Terry fell into deep depression and planned to kill himself, but God intervened. Upon visiting his burned-out property, Terry noticed a scorched scrap of paper from one of his wife's books leaning against a charred tree trunk. The page was about a man who lost his entire family in a car accident and he said.... *"[God,] I couldn't understand why You would take my family and leave me behind to struggle along without them. And I guess I still don't totally understand that part of it. But I do believe that You're sovereign; You're in control."* That page was like a direct message from God, and it turned Terry's life around.[9]

Terry chose to forgive and God has given him a new family. He travels the country speaking the powerful message of forgiveness in schools, churches and prisons.

Chapter 10. Forgive and Forget

It's with that attitude through Christ that you must look past the person that did you wrong and look to the Person who gave us the greatest example to follow... and forgive.

If you can't forgive your spouse, why would you expect God to forgive you?

> *"But if ye do not forgive, neither will your Father which is in heaven forgive your trespasses."* Mark 11:26

Forgiveness by Matthew West[10]

It's the hardest thing to give away
And the last thing on your mind today
It always goes to those that don't deserve

It's the opposite of how you feel
When the pain they caused is just too real
It takes everything you have just to say the word

Forgiveness, Forgiveness

It flies in the face of all your pride
It moves away the mad inside
It's always angers own worst enemy
Even when the jury and the judge
Say you gotta' right to hold a grudge
It's the whisper in your ear saying Set It Free

Forgiveness, Forgiveness

Show me how to love the unlovable
Show me how to reach the unreachable
Help me now to do the impossible

Forgiveness, Forgiveness

Help me now to do the impossible

Forgiveness

It will clear the bitterness away
It can even set a prisoner free
There is no end to what its power can do
So, let it go and be amazed

Marriage is a Four-Letter Word

By what you see through eyes of grace
The prisoner that it really frees is you

Forgiveness, Forgiveness

Show me how to love the unlovable
Show me how to reach the unreachable
Help me now to do the impossible

Forgiveness

I want to finally set it free
So show me how to see what Your mercy sees
Help me now to give what You gave to me

Forgiveness, Forgiveness

Forgetting

This is the tricky one. For many people it's easier to forgive than to forget. Forgiveness can be forced, without trying to forget it. Your spouse can say, *"I forgive you,"* yet still harbor bitterness and resentment inside.

Without learning and allowing yourself to forget, you will find yourself resurrecting issues that you supposedly forgave and put to rest years prior. So if you bring up a past failure long after it's supposedly forgiven, what does it speak about your type of forgiveness? It says... *"My forgiveness is not genuine but contingent upon you and what you do or say to misplace my trust."*

I'm glad God doesn't treat me like that. I'm glad He doesn't throw it up in my face and exclaim, *"You did it again Brian! Can't you do anything right?"* I'm so glad that I can turn to God and seek His forgiveness for something that I've said or done and He forgives me!

Chapter 10. Forgive and Forget

> *"If we confess our sins He* (God) *is faithful and just to forgive us our sins and cleanse us from all unrighteousness."* 1 John 1:9

Wow, what forgiveness! What love! When I fall flat on my face the next day, God doesn't bring it up that I did the same thing a day prior. He doesn't berate me like a Drill Sergeant or stick me on a time-out bench. Not only does He genuinely forgive, He genuinely forgets...and He does it purposely as part of His character!

> *"As far as the east is from the west, so far hath he removed our transgression from us."* Psalms 103:12

> **You'll never move forward into your destiny until you learn to forget your negative history**

If you want a loving, life-lasting marriage, then learn to forgive and forget. The Apostle Paul said, *"Forgetting those things which are behind, reaching forth unto those things which are before..."*[11]

You'll never move forward into your destiny until you learn to forget your negative history.

I had a respectable husband tell me, *"I forgive, BUT I'll never forget."* Got it. I understand that there's a part of your brain that won't ever forget but that attitude will only infect and negatively affect your marriage. All of what replays in your brain is directly connected with how you file it in your heart.

Forgiveness and forgetting are choices you make because you choose to do what you want to do. When you have the attitude, *"I'll never forget what you did to me,"* you are filing the pain in the depths of your heart and revisiting the file often in your brain. That's your choice - it's a safeguard to protect yourself from being hurt again. Forgiveness makes you vulnerable. It gives you nothing more to stand on and that was hard to do…but forcing forgetfulness….that's strips everything away!

When the pain of how you hurt begins to penetrate your thoughts, force it back into the file or, better yet, dump the file drawer at the foot of the cross and cry out for help. Remind yourself that you have already forgiven and therefore it's not to be a daily or weekly lunch for your brain.

Marriage is a Four-Letter Word

In 2008, I was twenty feet in a tree cutting down a limb with a chainsaw.[12]

As the branch began to topple over, one of its limbs swung back and struck the chainsaw that I was holding, driving the spinning blade deep into my left forearm, ripping flesh and bone. In just a fraction of a second, the searing blade cut out a chuck of skin and muscle all the way to the bone.

I immediately threw the chainsaw from the tree and swung to the ground. I yelled to my partner for a towel and off we went to the emergency room.

Later that evening, I returned home with stitches and some interesting pictures. I could have lost my arm, but the good Lord was watching over me.

For the next three days, the pain began to set in. My nerves began to grow back and over the next two weeks, the pain finally subsided altogether and the stitches removed.

Today, I have a scar that has healed quite well. I rarely think about the accident anymore, but for the first few days of the chainsaw attack, all I could do was think about it!

....

Forgiving and forgetting is much like an injury that leaves a permanent scar. The pain is deep and the damage is traumatic, and although it may heal, the scar lasts forever. When devastating circumstances enter a marital relationship because of a spouse, forgiveness and forgetting is possible. Let me say that again: Forgiving and forgetting is possible! [13]

IT'S A CHOICE.

It doesn't mean that everything is *fine and dandy*. Nor does it mean that the *sin* is acceptable, either. The wound it has caused could be bloody, painful, bone-chilling and traumatizing. You probably need to see a doctor, a pastor or a counselor who can help you out by sewing you up and giving you something to help with the pain.

Chapter 10. Forgive and Forget

There'll be a scar. It'll be red. It'll throb and be painful for a couple weeks. You may even think about it when that time of the year rolls around. Just give it time. The pain will become faint and the scab will heal.

One day, you'll be sitting on your porch with your spouse, sipping on ice tea and enjoying life. You'll look over at your spouse and you'll remember that big ol' scar. If you dwell upon those thoughts, the memories of heartache and pain will come right back. It's at that time when a mature spouse will close the file, sit back, breathe, relax and say, "It's forgiven. Let it go."[14]

Mr. Nelson had a serious and painful circulation problem in his leg but refused to allow the recommended amputation. As the pain grew worse, Nelson grew bitter. "I hate it!" he would mutter about the leg. At last, he relented and told his doctor, "I can't stand it anymore. I'm through with that leg. Take it off."

Surgery was scheduled immediately and the leg was removed. But Nelson suffered phantom limb pain of the worst degree. The wound healed, but he could feel the torturous pressure of the swelling of the muscles that were no longer there, and he had no prospect of relief. He had hated the leg with such intensity that the pain had unaccountably lodged permanently in his brain.

Even though Mr. Nelson's leg had been removed and the pain had been stopped, his brain tricked him into feeling the pain. Because he had lived in a constant state of pain and anger, his brain assumed that state as normal long after the actual pain was gone.

If you have ever been so bitter, hurt and angry that it was a constant state of being…you need to forgive and forget. No matter what you think you should do, say, feel or act…you need to forgive.

People will let you down, so forgive. Circumstances will steal your joy, so forgive. Satan will rob you of your peace, so forgive. Don't give the spiritual enemy what he wants – that's you to harbor bitterness and resentment inside. Be like Jesus Christ, allow Him to fill you and help you to forgive and forget.

Marriage is a Four-Letter Word

When little things remind you of the hurt, immediately dragging the luggage of pain, focus, force it away, forgive and let go.

The FAULTBOX

A couple married for 15 years began having their share of more-than-usual disagreements. They purposed to make their marriage work and agreed on an idea the wife had. For one month, they planned to drop slips into two "Fault boxes." The boxes would provide a place to let the other know about daily irritations.

The wife started immediately and was diligent in both her efforts and approach:

- "Left the top off the peanut butter jar."
- "Wet towel on the shower floor."
- "Dirty socks not placed in hamper."
- "Home late from work."
- "Didn't fill up the car with gas."
- "Forgot to wash the dishes as promised."
- On and on until the end of the month.

After dinner, at the end of the month, they exchanged boxes. The husband reflected on the many slips of paper reminding him what he had done wrong... over and over again. Then the wife opened her box and began reading. The notes of paper were all the same and the message on each slip was, "I love you!"

You see, the wife's world revolved around *her*. The husband's world revolved around her, too. You might say they were both in love with the same woman. She viewed his shortcomings as problematic towards her. And, although the husband saw his wife's failings, he was reminded of how much

Chapter 10. Forgive and Forget

Christ had forgiven her and how he should be more like Christ.

How often do we focus on what other people owe us, not on what we owe others? Your forgiveness of others must not be based on their actions toward you, but on the Lord's action toward you. He forgives and forgets – and so should you.

Free you and your spouse from the past by forgiving one another as Christ forgave you. Put away the guilt! Put down the grudge and learn to forget the past! You've carried it long enough and it's time to let it go. Let go and let God.

> **Let go and let God...**

Forgiveness is a choice so choose it. Forgetting is a process so accept it! Choose it for the good of your spouse and for the health of your marriage. Choose it for the sake of the relationship between you and the Lord.

Marriage is a Four-Letter Word

The purpose of this book was to equip you with helpful tools to keep the love alive in your marriage. Marriage truly takes work, and by now, you realize that the work you pour into it is well worth it. The *work* is second nature because when you love, you give. Your marriage is not a short sprint to the finish line. It's a life-lasting marathon of love.

As you seek to identify and eliminate problems in the years to come, I encourage you to build your foundation on the Lord Jesus Christ and continue to enhance your love for one another.

It is my prayer that this book and all of its contents and stories have been a blessing to you!

God bless you,

Brian T. Hargis

Proverbs 3:5-6

Index

CHAPTER 1. *Marriage is a Four-Letter Word*

1. Pastor Steve Thornhill, of South Dayton Baptist Church, Moraine, Ohio, is an example of someone who loves his job in the ministry and looks forward to it each day. Being a pastor is not so much work to him as it is a privilege to do what he loves to do – which is to reach out to other people with the love of God.

2. City ordinances for yard maintenance are common. As an example, the ordinance for the city of Tulsa, Oklahoma states that your grass cannot exceed 12'. Source: https://www.cityoftulsa.org.

3. Traditional marriage vows: *I,_____, take you_____, to be my (wife/husband), to have and to hold from this day forward, for better or for worse, for richer, for poorer, in sickness and in health, to love and to cherish; until death do us part.*

4. The requirement for witnesses to sign the marriage certificate is to authenticate that the bride and groom have made commitments, promises, and vows to each other. The witnesses are to hold the wedded couple *accountable* to their vows. The statement, *"If anyone can say otherwise as to why this man and woman should not wed, let him speak now or forever hold his peace"* has been removed from most wedding dialogue due to the fact that most couples have broken God's laws of abstinence, or have been previously divorced for non-biblical reasons (Ibid; Chapter 4, #1). Can you imagine how embarrassing it would be for someone to stand and say, "Yeah preacher! I know of a few reasons why this couple should not be married….."?

5. I first started rock-climbing in 1997 when assigned to ODA 955 (the Mountain Team) of Bravo Company, 2nd Battalion, 19th Special Forces Group (Airborne). Initial training took place at Colorado's Turkey Rock, Eleven Mile Canyon, Flat Irons, and the Garden of the Gods. Subsequent training included California's famous Joshua Tree, West Virginia's Seneca Rocks, Ohio's John Bryant State Park, Washington's Mt.

Rainer, Kosovo's Mt. Ljuboten, and Austria's Mt. Grossglockner.

6. Vertical rock climbing routes are graded as class five (5.0). Each level of difficulty is rated after that from zero to fifteen (0-15) with 15 being the most difficult. A 5.0 to 5.1 climb would be an extremely easy route, 5.2 to 5.4 routes are basic beginner routes that require little skill, and 5.11 to 5.15 are extremely difficult and reserved for experienced, professional climbers.

7. Lao-Tzu, a Chinese philosopher (604-531 BC).

8. See Colossians 1:14 & John 3.

9. See Galatians 5:22-23.

10. John 3:16 is often displayed on signs at United States sporting events. NFL quarterback Tim Tebow (Denver Broncos 20010-2011, and New York Jets 2012) routinely sported John 3:16.

11. See 1 Corinthians 13:13. The word "charity" is correctly translated in the Bible as a superior word than "love" because it reminds us that true love is given freely without any hope or expectation of receiving something in return.

12. See Chapter 6; Society's View of Marriage.

CHAPTER 2. *Identifying Problems*

1. Dr. Thomas Gresham (Ibid; Chapter 5, #12) once preached a sermon while wearing a plastic mask, thus demonstrating *plastic Christianity*.

2. "For what shall it profit a man, if he shall gain the whole world, and lose his own soul?" Mark 8:36

3. Counselor referred to in this context as a pastor or a Christian counselor, both of whom should offer advice from a Biblical perspective. In the context used here, I was both.

Index

4. U.S. Army Special Forces, the *Green Berets*.
   - Bravo Company, 2/19th SFG (A); 1995.
   - Special Forces Assessment and Selection (SFAS); 1995.
   - Special Forces Qualification Course (SFQC) (18C); 1996
   - Language school; French; 1997.
   - ODA 955; 1997- 2003.
   - Drill Sergeant; Dec. 2003 - June 2005.
   - Team Sergeant (18Z); 2005-2007.
   - Deployments and missions: Egypt, Iceland, Hungary, Kuwait, Kosovo, Serbia, Austria and Afghanistan.
5. See Psalms 18:20-24; 26:9-10; Proverbs 12:14; Ecclesiastes 2:11; 4:6; Isaiah 59:1-3.

CHAPTER 3. *Eliminating Problems*

1. A perfect, comical video to show that men are "solvers" and "fixers" but women just want you to listen is found on YouTube. Title: It's Not about the Nail.
2. It's true. Many of the men counseled for marital issues purposely delay in going home. Some hand out at the office or team room, some stop by the bar and some go to their deer stand.
3. *Attack* and *break contact* are military terms associated with Infantry tactics.
4. To *"hide your head in the sand"* is known as the ostrich effect. It comes from the legend that ostriches bury their heads in the sand to avoid danger. Reference: www.en.wikipedia.org/wiki/Ostrich_effect.
5. Source: Infante, D.A., & Wigley, C.J. (1986). "Verbal Aggressiveness: An Interpersonal Model and Measure." *Communication Monographs, 53*(1), p. 61-69.
6. Dayton Police Officer Roger Kielbaso (retired) and I were partners during the summer of 2001 accumulated more arrests than any other partnered team.

Marriage is a Four-Letter Word

7. Dwan Contreras (formerly Lerma) of El Paso, Texas, Chaplain Assistant (56M) assigned with me to the 10th MTN DIV (LI), 1st BCT, HHC, 1st BSTB; January 2009 to July 2010.

CHAPTER 4. *Marriage Killers*

1. Biblical reasons for divorce: see Matthew 19:1-9; Mark 10:11-12; 1 Corinthians 7:12-13.
2. Stated in the Christian film, *Facing the Giants*. (Ibid; Chapter 5, #20).
3. Both David and Paul made themselves happy and encouraged themselves in the Lord. David was about to be stoned by his own men, and Paul was in jail. See 1 Samuel 30:6 and Acts 26:2.
4. Michelle Romine-Barrette, Attorney.
5. Coach Dickens of Xenia Christian Academy, a ministry of Bible Baptist Church,1679 West Second Street, Xenia, Ohio 45385; 937-372-7804.
6. Evangelist David C. Spurgeon uses this expression on the cover of his Gospel tract known as the *Fast Lane*. For ordering information, contact Charity Baptist Church at 937-567-7929 or via the website: www.charitybaptist.org. Spurgeon's website: www.davidspurgeon.org.
7. A few months after writing this chapter, I went to the phone store and purchased a mount to hold my portable GPS. The package advertising it depicted an attractive Asian woman dressed in red leather, leaning on the hood of a red sports car. Interesting how items are advertised.
8. See John 8:1-11.
9. See "blush" in Jeremiah 6:15; 8:12 & Ezekiel 39:7.
10. Retired Chaplain (MAJ) Jeff Struecker, former U.S. Army Ranger, fought in the battle of Mogadishu in 1993; Operation Restore Hope. For more info, visit www.jeffstruecker.com.
11. The top-selling books of all time (2011):
    - The Bible: 6-7 billion*
    - *Harry Potter*: 400+ mil.

Index

- The Qur'an: 200+ mil.
- *A Tale of Two Cities*: 200+ mil.
- *The Hobbit*: 150+ mil.
- *The Lord of the Rings*: 150 mil.
- *The Book of Mormon*: 120 mil.
- *The Da Vinci Code*: 80 mil.
- *Left Behind*: 65 mil.
- *Webster's Dictionary*: 55 mil.
- *Anne of Green Gables*: 50 mil.
- *The Purpose Driven Life*: 30 mil. (Rick Warren).

*Claimed to be the most stolen book of all time by several sources: www.answebag.com; www.religiousnewsblog.com; www.woai.com; mylot.com; www.bibleprophecyupdate.com.

12. See *"out of the abundance of the heart,"* Matthew 12:34; Luke 6:45.

13. See Philippians 2:12-13.

CHAPTER 5. *Start Right, Stay Right, Finish Right*

---

1. Dr. Greg Estep is the founder of Charity Baptist Church in Kettering, Ohio, originally in Beavercreek, established in 1977. Estep is also the founder of Charity Baptist Bible Institute and Seminary (CBBI). Although retired in 2001, Estep is still an active part of both. Thomas Gresham served as pastor and president from 2001- 2014. Patrick Murphy is the current pastor and president (Ibid; Chapter 5, #12).

2. See 1 Thessalonians 4:3; 1 Corinthians 6:18; 7:2; 10:8; Acts 15:20, 25, 29; Ephesians 5:3; Colossians 3:5.

3. Associated press report; July 20, 2009, http://www.foxnews.com.

4. For *Renter* and *Owner* mentality description, see Chapter 1; Marriage is a Four-Letter Word; Marital Leasing, p.5.

5. *Drive thru weddings* are real and usually open until 3 a.m.! Las Vegas, Nevada (Sin City and also known as *"the entertainment capital of the world"*) has numerous drive-through Chapels. Packages range from $199 to $499. Source: www.chapelsoflasvegas.com.

Marriage is a Four-Letter Word

- Pigeon Forge, TN also has one: www.drivethruidos.com.
- Myrtle Beach, SC also has one: www.loverslanemyrtlebeach.com.

6. The States of Colorado and Montana allow for proxy marriages. I was first exposed to this in 2010 when on deployment in Afghanistan and a Soldier told me he just got married by proxy. The *official* $950 marriage ceremony is usually performed via the internet in the physical absence of either the bride or groom, as only one needs to be present in single proxy, but both may be absent in double proxy, as long as two *actors,* relatives, friends, or street bums stand in in your absence. Source: www.marriagebyproxy.com.

7. Common-law marriage, sometimes called *sui juris marriage*, is recognized in many states even though there is no legal marriage ceremony performed or civil marriage contract. Common-law marriages are legal in DC and the nine states of AL, CO, IW, KS, OK, RI, TX and SC. Note: There is no common-law divorce! See more at www.family- law.lawyers.com.

8. See Matthew 7:24-27.

9. Ruckman, Peter S., *The Ruckman Reference Bible*, 2nd Edition, Bible Baptist Bookstore, Pensacola, Florida, 2009. Website: www.kjv1611.org.

10. *"Born again"* is a Biblical term that was popularized by the *Flower Children* of the 1960s. It is a Biblical term that Jesus first used when talking to the Pharisee Nicodemus. All people are either born again or not born again. To be born again simply means that you have repented of your sins and accepted Jesus as your Saviour. See John 3:1-21 for the best explanation.

11. See Galatians 6:8.

12. Chaplain Thomas Gresham, Montgomery and Greene County (Ohio) Sheriff Chaplain. Gresham was the senior pastor of Charity Baptist Church, Bible Institute and Seminary (CBBI), in Kettering, Ohio, 2001-

Index

2013. I was the assistant pastor from September 2003 to January 2009. Gresham is a seminary graduate of Blue Ridge Bible Institute, now The Bible Doctrine Institute (TBDI) of Jacksonville, Florida, where Dr. David Peacock is the president.

13. Brigade General Willard (Bill) M. Burleson III made this quote to me while in Afghanistan. At that time BG Burleson was the Brigade Commander (Colonel) of the 1st Brigade Combat Team, 10th Mountain Division (LI), Fort Drum, NY. May 2011.

14. The events corresponding to this section are…

    - Filmed a portion of *History's Ultimate Warrior* at Ft. Harrison, Montana, 2007. The name was later changed to *The Deadliest Warrior* and aired in 2009, 2010 and 2011 on SPIKE TV. For more information, visit www.spike.com.

    - The tallest mountain in Austria is the Grossglockner (12,461'), summit was reached in 2001. Picture from left to right. Top row: Ron (deceased), Neil, Rick, Kraig. Bottom row: Andre (deceased) Rob, Brian, Dan.

    - Completed jumps 19-21 with the black team of the Golden Knights, Raeford DZ, Raeford, NC, 2007.

    - The *Rome to Road* was during a visit to Philippi, Greece in 2003 via Kavala. Also visited the *jail cell* of Paul and Silas (Acts 16:23-40), and the site where Lydia was baptized (Acts 16:14-15, 40).

    - The *treacherous mountain slopes* was along the border of Macedonia, and the only ski resort in the country of Kosovo, in the city of Brezovica, 2003.

    - The black bear was owned by Mr. Johnson of Columbus, Ohio, 1999.

Marriage is a Four-Letter Word

- The K-9 attack was during a demonstration while attending the Police Academy of Dayton, Ohio in 1999.
- The monkey was presented as a gift by a jungle tribe during a mission trip to Mindanao, Philippines in 2007. The endeavor was led by Evangelist Ebenezer Loquias and I was the first *white man* to visit the village. 70 precious souls were saved.
- The shark encounter was while snorkeling in the Florida Keys, 2007 and 2011 (not uncommon).

15. The *fight* with the chainsaw was self-inflicted (October 2008).
16. References:
    - Operation Resolute Support, Afghanistan: 2015.
    - Operation Enduring Freedom, Afghanistan: 2014.
    - Operation Enduring Freedom, Afghanistan: 2010-2011.
    - Mission trips, Philippines: 2005, 2006, 2008.
    - Mission trips, Mexico: 2004, 2006, 2007, 2013.
    - Operation Bright Star, Egypt: 1993.
    - Operation Northern Viking, Iceland: 1999.
    - SF exchange mission, Serbia: 2007. One of the first US soldiers to perform a military parachute jump in Serbia. Awarded Serbian jump wings by their President, Boris Tadic.
17. We make judgments of people every day. Judging motive is different from judging sin. The most misquoted verse of the Bible is Matthew 7:7 about "Judge not." We are to judge sin (1 Corinthians 2:15; 5:3). We are to separate from evildoers and *mark* heretics (Philippians 3:17; 2 Corinthians 6:17).
18. King David; see 2 Samuel 11 & 12. Just Lot; see 2 Peter 2:7. Rahab; see Joshua 2-6; Heb. 11:31; Woman at the well; see John 4. Peter; see Acts 2-3. Jesus reading minds; see Matthew 9:4; 12:25; 15:19, etc.
19. A quote from Dr. Greg Estep (see Ch. 5, note 1). Often repeated when speaking on the subject of hopelessness.
20. *Fireproof,* a Christian movie produced in 2008 by Sherwood Baptist Church in Albany, Georgia on a $500,000 budget that grossed millions. It's about a married couple that experienced problems to the brink of

Index

divorce only to get the help they needed from a unique source.

- *The Love Dare* book can be purchased separately (or in a kit) as a devotional guide that will lead your heart back to truly loving your spouse. For more information, visit www.fireproofmymarriage.com and www.lovedarebook.com.
- *Facing the Giants*, *Flywheel* and *Courageous* were also produced by Sherwood Baptist Church.

21. *The Five Love Languages* by Dr. Gary Chapman is a book written to help you learn the "language" that both you and your spouse use so that you can communicate effectively together. See www.5lovelanguages.com.

22. See Ephesians 5:22-25; 6:1.

CHAPTER 6. *Society's View of Marriage*

1. Sources: Lewanika, Sandi M., How To Continue Parenting After Getting a Divorce (http://www.associatedcontent.com, November 11, 2009); Haas, Rebekah, A Closer Look at the Reasons for the High American Divorce Rate; http:// www.associatedcontent.com, February 23, 2007; www.divorcerate.com; www.sound -divorce-advice.info.com;(accessed December 1, 2010)

2. Olson, Jeremy, More Couples Say 'Yes' to Living Together (*Minneapolis Star Tribune*: Stars and Stripes, October 18, 2010) p.9; Riley, Jennifer, Co-Habitation in America (www.christianpost.com, September 26, 2010).

3. Yen, Hope, Study: 4 in 10 Say Marriage Becoming Obsolete in U.S. (*Stars and Stripes*, November 19, 2010) p.6.

4. Source: www.unmarried.org/housing.

5. Definition of *Hate Speech:* speech that attacks, threatens or insults a person or group on the basis of national origin, ethnicity, color, religion, gender, gender identity, sexual orientation or disability. This is the world's accepted definition from the dictionary, February 1, 2015. Source: www.dictionary.reference.com/browse/hate+speech

Marriage is a Four-Letter Word

6. See 1 Corinthians 7:37; 15:58; Hebrews 3:14; 6:19, etc.

7. See John 14:6.

8. See Romans 1.

9. Source: www.cleveland.com/nation/index.ssf/2010

10. Source: www.cbsnews.com/stories/2009/09/24

11. Source: www.nationmaster.com and http://www.divorcemagazine.com.

12. Source: U.S. Census Bureau, Statistical Abstract of the United States: 2003; U.S. Census Bureau, 1900-1950, U.S. Census of Population: 1950, Vol. II, Part 1; 1960, U.S. Census of Population: 1960, Vol. I; 1970, U.S. Census of Population: 1970, Vol. I, Part 1; 1980, U.S. Census of Population: 1980, Vol. I, Part 1; 1990, U.S. Census of Population: 1990, General Population Characteristics, (CP-1-1); Census 2000 Summary File (SF3); Current Population Reports, America's Families and Living Arrangements: 2000, Series P20-537, and earlier reports.

13. Yen, Hope, Study: 4 in 10 Say Marriage Becoming Obsolete in U.S. (*Stars and Stripes*, November 19, 2010) p.6.

14. Source: www.foxnews.com (June 2, 2010).

15. Source: www.encylopedia.wickipedia.org (most expensive divorces).

16. Evangelist Philip Schipper of BIG Ministries – serving a BIG God. Phil made this quote at the Family Conference hosted in February of 2010, Fort Drum, NY. *"Marriage - Something Worth Fighting For"* was the theme. For more information on Schipper, see www.philschipper.com.

CHAPTER 7. *The Missing Family Table*

1. See Acts 1:14; 2:1-47.

2. Reference: *Are Americans Still Serving Up Family Dinners?* Source: www.harrisinteractive.com/NewsRoom/HarrisPolls/tabid.

3. Strategies for keeping clutter off your dining table. Sources: www.unclutterer.com and www.motherearthnews.com.

Index

4. Larry Clayton taught me much about interacting with the family during our time of deployment in Afghanistan 2010-2011.

5. See Ephesians 5:22-33 and Genesis 2:20-25.

6. See 1 Peter 3.

7. See Ephesians 5:21-25; 6:1-2.

8. Dr. Claro Loquias Sr. was the inspiration and planter of hundreds of churches throughout the island of Mindanao, Philippines. Hundreds of preachers have been trained and sent out through the Bible College, under the discipleship of himself and his Evangelistic sons, Ebenezer and Kim Loquias. Countless lives have been forever changed as the result of one man that was totally surrendered to God. Dr. Loquias graduated to heaven on April 24, 2012.

9. Known as *The Lord's Prayer*. See Luke 11:1-4.

10. See Genesis 3:17; The curse is not lifted until Isaiah 11:1-9 & Romans 8:19-22.

11. Ibid; Chapter 6, #16.

CHAPTER 8. *Improving the Marital Foxhole*

1. This was the very first chapter, written during Operation Enduring Freedom in Afghanistan 2010. It was originally going to be titled *"Chaplain's Marital Tips"* for the unit's Facebook page during the unit's deployment.

2. *"Contender or Pretender?"* was the title of a sermon preached by Dr. Thomas Gresham, Charity Baptist Church, Kettering, Ohio (Ibid; Chapter 4, #12).

3. *"War is Hell"* - Stated by General William Tecumseh Sherman at the Michigan Military Academy on June 19, 1879. In 1945, President Harry S. Truman said, *"Sherman was wrong. I'm telling you I find peace in hell."*

4. See James 4:1

Marriage is a Four-Letter Word

5. Ibid; Chapter 6, #16.

6. 1 Peter 3

7. N.Y. ADC. LAW 16-118: NY Code - Section 16-118: Littering prohibited.

    1) No person shall litter, sweep, throw or cast, or direct, suffer or permit any servant, agent, employee, or other person under his or her control to litter, sweep, throw or cast any ashes, garbage, paper, dust or other rubbish and refuse of any kind whatsoever, in or upon any street or public place, vacant lot, air shaft, areaway, backyard court or alley.

    2) The violation of any provision of this section shall constitute an offense punishable by a fine of not less than fifty dollars nor more than two hundred fifty dollars, or by imprisonment not to exceed ten days or both.

8. Citizen Arrests are still authorized. The District of Columbia Law 23-582(b) reads as follows: A private person may arrest another: – (1) who he has probable cause to believe is committing in his presence – (a) a felony, or (b) an offense enumerated in section 23-581, etc. Reference: www.constitution.org/grossack/arrest. The police department in Arroye Grande, California, offers this helpful four-step guide to making a citizen's arrest. Reference: www.arroyogrande.org.

9. See Chapter 2, Identifying Problems.

10. Ibid; Chapter 6, #16.

11. Source: www.covenanteyes.com.

12. *"She girdeth her loins with strength, and strengtheneth her arms."* Proverbs 31:17.

13. FOX News: Global Sex Survey; October 31, 2006.

14. *"It is good for a man not to touch a woman."* 1 Corinthians 7:1b.

15. The Associated Press: New survey tells how much sex we're having (MSNBC report; June 22, 2007). 16% of adults first had sex before the age of 15, while only 15% abstained from sex until at least age 21. Couples that engage in sex before marriage are candidates most likely

Index

not to have sex on their wedding night due to stress associated with planning and the weariness of the day's events. Couples who have not engaged in sex before marriage have something to look forward to on that special occasion.

16. Read what Jesus says about adultery in the heart; see Matthew 5:27-28.
17. Source: www.mplscounseling.com/affairs-and-cheating/affairs-in-the-workplace.
18. Source: http://athomedad.org/media-resources/statistics.

CHAPTER 9. *Reasonable Rules for Raising Rug Rats*

1. Dr. Humberto Gomez Cabellaro Sr., pastor and missionary in Mexico, made this statement while preaching at CBC, Beavercreek, Ohio. Humberto has translated the Bible into the most recent and purest Spanish translation – the RVG 2010. Reference: www.reinavaleragomez.com. Picture taken in Mexico, 2013.

2. Co-sleeping made it into the dictionary. Although a controversial subject in the United States, families are accustomed to bed-sharing in other countries. I noticed that it was very acceptable in the Philippines, and in countries with one- bedroom homes.

3. Sleeping disorders can become an unusual, obsessive behavior, such as sleeping with a hair dryer. Source: *My Strange Addiction*, Author Kim Carollo, December 2010. Reference: http://www.abcnews.go.com.

4. Study conducted by Harris Interactive (Rochester, NY), July 2005. Reference: www.petage.com.

5. Taphephobia. Reference: www.medterms.com, and www.wikio.com featuring video starring Bob Newhart, August 8, 2009.

6. List of snowboarding terms and definitions can be found at

Marriage is a Four-Letter Word

www.snowboarding.com.

7. Months after writing this chapter, I returned from deployment and coached Izak's t-ball team for the next season. Talk about learning patience! I learned the primary reason why they don't keep score for 1st Grade t-ball is because it is chaotic. Just trying to teach them the basic fundamentals of the game is difficult, let alone keeping statistics and score.

8. Jordan Hargis has become quite an accomplished musician and has led congregational singing at worship services in Fort Polk, LA and Fort Bragg, NC.

9. For more information about Ritchie Moody and/or baseball lessons, visit www.rmbaseball.com or call 937-604-3455.

10. The *Guinness World Records* book states that Nolan Ryan holds the record for the fastest pitch ever thrown, recorded at 108.1 mph in 1974. Reference: www.efastball.com.

11. See John 1:1-14 and I John 2:15-17.

12. Dr. Jack Patterson made this statement in July of 2003 at Charity Baptist Camp Meeting, Beavercreek, Ohio. Obviously not an original statement, but still one worth living by! Dr. Patterson is the president and founder of Reclamation Ranch in Empire, Alabama, a boarding school for troubled girls 12-17 years of age and young men ages 18-35. Reference: www.reclamationranch.com.

13. Ibid; Chapter 5, #10.

14. MLG, known as Major League Gaming, founded in 2002, holds official video game tournaments throughout the world. The competitors are composed mainly of adult men who compete as a career, some making millions of dollars in prizes. See www.majorleaguegaming.com.

15. My grandfather, Charles Hargis, 86, graduated to Heaven on January 02, 2011. He never was able to see this book, but he left a legacy of moral and spiritual characteristics that were passed down to three

Index

generations. We love you, Grandpa.

16. Next on the calendar is the *rapture* of the church; I Thessalonians 4:13-18; I Corinthians 15:51-54; Acts 1; not to be confused with the Second Coming (Advent) of Christ; I Thessalonians 5; Revelations 19, etc.

17. Tony Hawk is an American professional skateboarder, building more than 400 skateboard parks throughout the United States. Reference: www.tonyhawk.com.

18. Stated by Evangelist David Spurgeon, December 16, 2004 at an Evangelists Meeting, Beavercreek, Ohio. For more information about David Spurgeon, visit www.davidspurgeon.org.

19. "Ministers" refers to ordained pastors, missionaries, evangelists, Chaplains, teachers and preachers within the body of Christ.

20. Stated on March 26, 2005, in a sermon by Tom Gresham at Charity Baptist Church, Kettering Ohio. Gresham is the current pastor of Liberty Baptist Church, Moraine, Ohio. Reference: www.libertybaptistdayton.com.

CHAPTER 10. *Forgive and Forget*

1. See 1 John 4:7-8.
2. "Three strikes and you're out!"
3. SDCC (the Self-Defense Combat Course) was created in 2001 and continues to be taught primarily in churches. An advanced SDCC is taught to elite military units and incorporates the style of Bill Wolfe's Modern Defendo and the original OSS. Reference: www.whwolfe.com. For availability and course information, contact the author by writing to Brian Hargis
   - E-mail: brianhargis1@gmail.com or brian.hargis1@us.army.mil
4. See Luke 23:34.

Marriage is a Four-Letter Word

5. God loves us so much that He sent His only begotten Son to die on the cross for sin (John 3:16) and God calls us to salvation. He hates sin and He is angry at the wicked everyday (Psalms 7:11) for their rejection of Jesus Christ and their preponderance of sin. Unless they repent and turn to Him (Luke 13:3) they will be cast into Hell (Psalms 9:17). If you do not have Jesus as your Lord and Savior, repent of your sins, call upon Him and ask for forgiveness (Romans 10:9-13).
6. See 1 Corinthians 5:17.
7. See Psalm 103:14.
8. See Hebrews 12.
9. Terry Caffey has appeared on numerous programs including 20/20 with Barbara Walters and Dr. Phil. In 2013 I met Terry Caffey at Fort Hope Baptist Church in Leesville, LA through Pastor Keary Jordan. Both Terry and Keary are great men of God. Visit Terry's website at www.terrycaffey.com.
10. *Forgiveness* is a song written by Christian musician Matthew West. It's a true story about Renee Napier, a mother whose daughter was killed by a drunk driver named Eric whom she forgave. This an amazing story with video that can be watched on YouTube and at www.mattewwest.com.
11. See Philippians 3:13.
12. Injury occurred in October of 2008.
13. I've counseled and helped numerous couples with forgiving and forgetting. Couples that were in serious trouble due to infidelity, addictions and abuse. Help can be achieve by putting the Lord in the center and working hard to forgive and forget. The spouse that sinned must truly be repentive and pour 100% into building trust back into the relationship. The spouse that forgives must work hard at keeping the file in check. Most importantly, it takes time. If you fit this category, don't give up! Seek help and put the Lord in the middle of the circumstances.
14. **"Let It Go"** is a song from Disney's 2013 animated feature film *Frozen*.

CPSIA information can be obtained
at www.ICGtesting.com
Printed in the USA
FFOW04n0544060415
12336FF